Contents

Introduction

'We are all held in a loving, accepting gaze ...
what difference will it make to our relationships with
others if we believe we are all held in the same loving regard?'[1]

These materials have been written in the light of appalling statistics for teenage pregnancies and rising rates of sexually transmitted infections (STIs) in young people. At present, Britain has the highest rate of teenage pregnancies in Europe, at 27 per 1000,[2] the most common STI, Chlamydia, has seen a 150% rise over the past ten years.[3]

Meanwhile the DCSF's *Sex and Relationships Education Guidance for 2010* contains clear recommendations about a needed shift in emphasis; sexuality should be taught within relationships and a diversity of beliefs and lifestyles should be explored.[4] The Children's Society have published *A Good Childhood: Searching for Values in a Competitive Age,* a report about children's contemporary experiences of growing up, which makes strong recommendations about the way sex education should be taught.[5]

Love and Sex Matters hopes to offer a path that will deliver the recommendations of the DSCF's *Sex and Relationships Education Guidance* within a framework of Christian values and is offered as a response to suggestions made in *A Good Childhood.* The emphasis in these materials is on creating dialogue through activity that will help children and young people grow in emotional articulacy and develop the self-esteem to navigate a personal life that honours both themselves and others.

'Excessive individualism ...
commercial and peer pressures encourage risky lifestyles.'[6]

These materials also aim to help young people open their eyes to how media and advertising place human sexuality and relationships within the realm of consumerism, so removing the spirituality from intimacy. These lessons aim to help children and young people to reject the advertising pressures for conformity in beauty and, instead, realise their own wonder and worth as unique and beautiful people. Thus, good self-esteem is presented as a necessary foundation for building mutually satisfying and beneficial relationships. *Love and Sex Matters* also seeks to question the media representation that teenage sexual activity is, or should be, the norm.

'As sex can create human beings, sex education should be treated with seriousness and it should centre on love and responsibility within the context of family life.'[7]

These materials do not offer one Christian moral path, such as abstinence before marriage; however, they do seek to present that path as a positive, viable life choice and uphold the importance of marriage and family life.

In several of the lessons, students are asked to consider a variety of Christian, other faith, agnostic and atheist perspectives on issues of relationships and sexuality. They are then encouraged to use these perspectives to discuss their own ideas, with the emphasis on developing emotional articulacy.

'There is more involved than the defence of traditional family patterns – unless believers can show all of us ways of handling the education of emotion and of preparing people for adult commitment in relationships, all that will be seen is an agenda of anxiety, censoriousness and repression.'[8]

It is hoped that through these materials children and young people will be encouraged to ponder the profound significance and meaning of sex and consider the spirituality of relationships. Although this resource has been written with church schools in mind, the teaching ethic and multi-faith approach are such that it can also make a rich contribution to sex and relationships education outside this context.

At a time of changing family patterns and parental stress overload, there are many youngsters seeking the love, attention, security and identity that may not have been afforded them as a foundational experience. As a result sexual and emotional needs, love and relationships, often get confused, conflated and entangled. Many children and young people in our schools are not given the opportunity to discuss and formulate a language to articulate their feelings and needs either at home or in other contexts. They are not, therefore, being offered a safe environment in which to decide upon a meaningful sexual ethic for themselves, one that will give them the guidelines for their life. In this way, we are not protecting the young in our care and we are not helping them to live 'life in all its fullness'.

All schools, and in particular church schools, have a responsibility to love, serve and protect the children and young people they are educating. These materials seek to help children in today's world to find their own course through the smorgasbord of modern sexuality. This is offered against the backdrop of a belief in the unconditional love of God for all and the grace of God's forgiveness.

Kate Guthrie, Verity Holloway & Katy Staples
February 2010

In summary

Love and Sex Matters aims to:

- Offer exciting, fun and interactive lessons.
- Give opportunities to rehearse appropriate language and develop articulacy.
- Build self-esteem and high regard for others; in church schools this is rooted in a belief that all are loved by God.
- Uphold the sanctity of marriage, the importance of long-term relationships and stable family life.
- Offer abstinence before marriage as a valid life choice to be taken seriously while respecting people and their life choices.
- Offer views from a variety of Christian perspectives, from other faiths and from non-religious life perspectives.
- Enable children and young people to question messages in the media and advertising about body image and sexuality.
- Offer a starting point that does not assume teenage sexual activity as the norm.
- Create opportunities for children and young people to explore the deeper questions as to the meaning and significance of the sexual act in relationships.
- Invite a holistic consideration of sexuality that takes it beyond just the physical and explores the emotional, spiritual and moral aspects of sexuality: more than an exploration of bodily changes at puberty and 'how to put a condom on a banana'.
- Be realistic in understanding the raging power and force of sexuality.
- Acknowledge the complex context of the modern world in which today's children and young people find themselves.
- Be accessible to those of all faiths and none.
- Recognise each person's intrinsic worth and value.
- Allow consideration of human relationships as part of the greater love of God.
- Offer a vision of sacred committed relationships where personal and spiritual growth and mutual support can flourish.

Creating a classroom climate for good relationships and sex education

It is intended that these materials will help children and young people develop emotional articulacy and confidence in discussing relationships. They are not DVD/worksheet factual lessons although these lessons can be used in conjunction with materials such as the Channel 4 DVD *Living & Growing*, which is recommended by many local authorities.

These lessons do require teachers to be comfortable with managing discussion about matters that may be of a sensitive nature, and they are best used after appropriate training.

These are materials that seek active learning and debate and therefore could be deemed risky by some. There are teachers who may find the open discussion of issues relating to relationships and sexuality too sensitive to handle easily. Although ideally relationships are best discussed by the class teacher, it may, in certain circumstances, be appropriate to offer support and allow lessons to be taught by a member of staff more comfortable with handling sensitive issues.

Several of the lessons include a variety of opinions from religious and non-religious perspectives. They are not intended to be the definitive orthodoxy for any faith and the inclusion of the huge range of different opinions within all faiths and non-religious life perspectives has been difficult to reflect fully. The range of opinions offered is merely intended to reflect the diversity of views held by representative (fictional) young people. The aim is that children and young people will reflect on those opinions in order to help them develop their own ethics/beliefs.

It may be worth saying that opinions for discussion should be selected not only on the basis of the age of the pupils, but also on the needs of the group. We have given simpler versions of some opinion worksheets for younger children, which means that a teacher can select which will be most appropriate for a group, or even give some small groups in a class the standard worksheet, and other groups the simpler worksheet. It would still be possible to have a whole-class discussion afterwards. There are also some extension questions for abler children. Teachers can further tailor the resources for their group by limiting the number of examples, and selecting only examples from the most appropriate faith/belief perspectives.

Some classes may find issues to do with relationships and sexuality embarrassing, sensitive and very exciting! This situation can lead to defensive and heightened behaviour such as giggling, silliness or protracted silence. Strategies to cope with these behaviours need to be developed. Teachers as far as possible need to model behaviour that shows the normality of the discourse, that there is no reason to be embarrassed or silly.

Teachers may wish to establish ground rules for behaviour to ensure good sensitive listening and an appreciation of each other's ideas without criticism – however it is likely that these are already a part of the culture of the school. Teachers need to praise and value each verbal contribution made in order to encourage the more reticent to know that it is a safe space.

Handling pupil questions: teaching SRE in partnership with the home

It is important that pupils can ask questions in a safe environment – however, there is no obligation for a teacher to answer every question. Pupils may ask questions that are not relevant to the curriculum appropriate for that age group; this may be to shock or in order to gain kudos. Answering such questions may lead discussion into an inappropriate area, one that may not meet with the approval of the governing/parent body.

It is quite acceptable for a teacher to respond to an inappropriate pupil question by explaining that it addresses an issue that pupils will cover when older and suggesting that the pupil ask someone at home in the meantime.

This type of answer protects the childhood latency of pupils in the class whilst not totally quashing the enquiry, and shares the responsibility for relationships/sex education with the parents or carers.

Some schools find the use of a question box useful. Asking pupils to put their questions into a box gives teachers an opportunity to filter out the less appropriate questions before answering. Teachers can explain that they will only answer questions that are appropriate for the class. It can also be suggested that if a pupil's question is not read out and answered, the pupil can ask someone at home or speak to the teacher directly.

Child Protection

When discussing relationship and sexuality issues in the classroom, a teacher may discover the inappropriate sexualisation of a pupil, or a disclosure could be made. Staff must know the school's processes for child protection before teaching this material.

Adapting the material to your local context

Some material included is potentially very sensitive. Depending on your local context it may be that, due to the make up of your pupil/parent/governing body, it is particularly pertinent to include the teaching of a particular issue for any given year group or indeed to omit it.

1. Rowan Williams quoted in Mike Highton, *Difficult Gospel: The Theology of Rowan Williams* (SCM Press: Canterbury, 2004), p.19.
2. Dunn, J. & Layard, Richard, *A Good Childhood: Searching for Values in a Competitive Age* (Penguin: London, 2009). 'Report Summary: Friends' available online: http://www.childrenssociety.org.uk/all_about_us/how_we_do_it/the_good_childhood_inquiry/report_summaries/14748.html [accessed 17 June 2009].
3. Avert.org, STD Statistics for the UK. [online] (updated 20 February 2009) Available at http://www.avert.org/stdstatisticuk.htm [accessed 22 June 2009].
4. Sir Alasdair Macdonald, Independent Review of the Proposal to Make Personal, Social, Health and Economic (PSHE) Education Statutory (Department for Children, Schools and Families: London, 2009) Available online at: http://publications.dcsf.gov.uk/default.aspx?PageFunction= productdetails&PageMode=publications&Productid=D SCF-00495-2009& [accessed 31 January 2010].
5. Dunn & Layard, *A Good Childhood.*
6. Dunn & Layard, *A Good Childhood.* p.4.
7. Dunn & Layard, *A Good Childhood,* p.49.
8. Rowan Williams quoted in Dunn & Layard, *A Good Childhood,* p.178.
9. *The Bible,* New International version (Zondervan: Michigan, 1978), John 10:10.

Overview

Lesson	Summary	Learning Outcomes
1. Making me; sexuality and the media	Pupils will think about the role of the media in shaping perceptions of sexuality and how it does this.	• I can explain how an advert uses sex to make me want to buy the product. • I can explain why the way the media works can be seen to devalue people.
2. My world, your world	Pupils will reflect on what love is and how love can be shown. They will consider what characteristics are needed to build long-lasting relationships.	• I can begin to describe what love is and explain several ways of showing someone you love him/her. • I can explain the qualities that a person needs to develop in order to build good, lasting relationships.
3. Firm foundations	Pupils will think about the benefits and difficulties of marriage, reflecting on the impact marriage has on the individual, the couple, the family and the wider community. Pupils will think about the emotional and spiritual aspects of sex and how these relate to a dating relationship.	• I can explain why Christians believe marriage to be a good thing for the people involved and the community of which they are a part married. • I can give reasons why some people decide to co-habit, whilst others decide to get married.
4. Great expectations?	Pupils will reflect on the emotional and spiritual significance and meaning of sex. They will consider what makes dating relationships special and why it is important to be careful with whom you make yourself open and vulnerable.	• I can suggest reasons why sex can be a meaningful and loving act. • I can suggest reasons why some young people become sexually active early. • I can describe what Christianity and other world religions believe to be significant about sex.
5. Contraception	Pupils will learn about the different types of contraception, as well as considering ethical questions associated with their use. Pupils will think about the meaning of sex and why it is best kept for marriage or long-term relationships.	• I can name 3–5 types of contraception and explain how they work. • I can explain what Christianity and other world religions think about contraception
6. Risky choices	Pupils will think about the health risks (STIs) of sleeping with strangers) and the role drugs and alcohol play in sexual assault. They also consider briefly the laws about sex.	• I can name 3–5 STIs. • I can explain the risks associated with using drugs and alcohol. • I can explain what the laws about sex are and why they are there.
7. Why wait?	Pupils will reflect on the stages of maturity and then think about the application of the material from the lessons 4–6.	• I can describe the stages of growing up • I can give someone advice on whether or not to become sexually active, based on my knowledge of the emotional, spiritual and physical aspects of sex.
8. Summary activities	Activities to draw the course together and encourage pupils to reflect on what they have learnt.	• I can consider how sex can be 'life-giving' or 'life-limiting'. • I can describe actions that would make my relationships more 'life-giving'.

Social and Emotional Aspects of Learning (SEAL) outcomes

SELF AWARENESS	Whole course	1. Making me; sexuality and the media	2. My world, your world	3. Firm foundations	4. Great expectations?	5. Contraception	6. Risky choices	7. Why wait?
Knowing myself								
1. I know that I am a unique individual and can think about myself on many different levels	■	■			■			
5. I can identify what is important for me and what I expect from myself, taking into account the beliefs and expectations that others have of me	■			■		■	■	■
6. I can reflect on my actions and identify lessons to be learned from them	■		■				■	
7. I can make sense of what has happened to me in my life and understand that things that come from my own history can make me prone to being upset or angry for reasons others may find difficult to understand					■			
Understanding my feelings								
8. I know and accept what I am feeling and can label my feelings	■		■					
10. I can be assertive when appropriate	▣				■		▣	■
11. I can recognise conflicting emotions and manage them in ways that are appropriate								
12. I can use my knowledge and experience of how I think, feel and respond, to choose my own behaviour, plan my learning and build positive relationships with others	■		■	■	■			■

▣ Grey denotes major themes

■ Black denotes minor themes

Making me: sexuality and the media

Lesson 1

In this lesson pupils will learn to assess critically the way in which the media shapes perceptions of sexuality. They will reflect, by analysing the role of sexuality in advertising, on how sex has been made into a consumer item. They will consider what fears this plays on and how it contributes to their expectations of sex. Pupils will then think about Christian, Buddhist and atheist reactions to the media and how these help a critical assessment of and response to the workings and impact of the media.

Learning Objectives
- Consider and critically assess the role of the media in shaping perceptions of sexuality, particularly within advertising.
- Reflect on the morality of the way the media works.

Learning Outcomes
- I can explain how an advert uses sex to make me want to buy the product.
- I can explain why the way the media works can be seen to devalue people.

Lesson Activities and Resources
- Introduction: Opening advert (10 minutes)
  - Adverts from teen magazines (not included)
- Playing the media (25 minutes)
  - Photos of products (not included)
  - Worksheet 1.1 *Spirituality, sexuality, media*
- Plenary (10 minutes)
  - Dove campaign for real beauty advert (not included, optional)

PSHE Curriculum
This lesson covers:
2.1.a. Pupils should be able to reflect critically on their own and others' values.
3.a. A study of personal wellbeing should include examples of diverse values encountered in society and the clarification of personal values.

Introduction - Opening advert
10 minutes - Whole class activity

Preparation: You will need an advert that implicitly or explicitly uses sexuality to sell a product, such as an advert for Lynx, DKNY, FCUK products, or many perfume adverts.

- Put an advert on the board, and ask the pupils to discuss the advert in pairs, considering the following questions:
  - What is the advert for? Describe what you see in the advert.
  - How does the advert try to sell the product?
  - What techniques are the advertisers using to persuade you to buy the product?
- Feedback to the class, rounding up the discussion with the question:
  - In what way is sexuality used to make you want to buy the product?

Playing the media
25 minutes - Small group activity

Preparation: Each small group will need a picture of a product, e.g. deodorant/perfume, shampoo, car, jewellery, jeans, or a computer game.

- Give each small group a picture of a product and give them ten minutes to make up a thirty-second spoof advert for their product, thinking about:
  - What might advertisers want to make you *fear* will happen if you do not have this product?
  - What qualities or other things might the product give you?
  - In what way might sexuality be used to make you want to buy the product?
- Ask the groups to perform their adverts to the class.

Spirituality, sexuality, media
15 minutes - Small group activity

Preparation: Each small group will need a copy of worksheet 1.1: *Spirituality, sexuality, media*.

- Give each group a copy of worksheet 1.1: *Spirituality, sexuality, media*.
- Ask pupils to use the statements to help them answer the questions.
- Feedback to the class, starting discussion with questions:
  - With which statements do you agree/disagree?

Extension questions

- Do you have to accept the messages given out by adverts? Is it possible to not accept them?
- How do you think adverts manipulate you to make you want to buy the product? How do you feel about this?

Plenary
10 minutes - Whole class activity

- If you have access to the internet, show the video 'Evolution', available from the Dove Campaign For Real Beauty website:
  http://www.campaignforrealbeauty.com/home_films_evolution_v2.swf
  Use this to start a discussion about the 'truthfulness' of adverts:
  - What does this clip tell you about how adverts are made?
  - How do you think adverts influence our idea of how we ought to look?
- If you do not have access to the internet, you can write the following quote on the board as a discussion-starter:
  'We don't influence 11–14 year olds, we own them.'
  Mr Johnstone, director of MTV
  - Do you think the media owns you? Why/why not?
  - To what extent do you think the media affects our ideas about what is sexually attractive?

Worksheet 1.1: *Spirituality, sexuality, media*

The following statements are beliefs held by some Christians, Buddhists and atheist.
Can you use these statements to help you answer the questions below?

'Your body is a temple of the Holy Spirit who lives in you. Your body is a gift from God, so it is not your own. To show respect to God, you must look after your body well.'

paraphrase of 1
Corinthians 6 vv.19–20

'Advertising makes people seem like objects and stops us seeing everyone as a unique person.'

paraphrase of Jean Kilbourne,
Beauty and the Beast of Advertising

'Sexual intimacy, where two people become one within marriage, is holy. The way sex is presented in the media rarely shows this.'

'Desire causes suffering or dissatisfaction with your life, which Buddhists call *dukkha*. Advertising is about making you want to buy things you do not have. So advertising can encourage a sense of dissatisfaction.'

'If I believed what adverts say, I would think everybody is out there having lots of good sex with their skinny, beautiful, smooth-skinned partners. Adverts lie.'

- Why might a Buddhist think that advertising is bad?
- How does presenting people as objects stop us valuing ourselves?
- What does Christianity say about the value of our bodies and sex?
- How is this different from what the media says?
- Which of the above opinions do you agree/disagree with? Why?

My world, your world

In this lesson, pupils will consider what love is and how to love other people. The different sorts of love in human relationships will be considered, as well as how love can be expressed. In this way, pupils will be helped to cultivate a language for expressing their emotions. Pupils will reflect on what characteristics provide a solid foundation for friendships and relationships.

Learning Objectives
- Consider ways love can be shown and learn how to express this emotion.
- Reflect on what character traits will help build strong relationships/friendships.

Learning Outcomes
- I can begin to describe what love is and explain several ways of showing someone you love him/her.
- I can explain the qualities that a person needs to develop in order to build good, lasting relationships.

Lesson Activities and Resources
- Introduction: Different types of love (15 minutes)
  - Worksheet 2.1: *Different types of love*
- Languages of love (20 minutes)
  - Worksheet 2.2: *Five love languages*
- Love is… (15 minutes)
  - Worksheet 2.3: *1 Corinthians 13: double bubble*
  - Worksheet 2.4: *1 Corinthians 13: blank double bubble*
- Plenary: Firm foundations (10 minutes)
  - Worksheet 2.5: *Firm foundations*

PSHE Curriculum
This lesson covers:
2.1.b. Pupils should be able to reflect on personal strengths, achievements and areas for development.
2.3.a. Pupils should be able to use social skills to build and maintain a range of positive relationships.
3.i. The study of personal wellbeing should include different types of relationships, including those within families and between older and young people, boys and girls, and people of the same sex, including civil partnerships.

Introduction - Different types of love
15 minutes - Whole class activity

Note to teachers

In this activity pupils are asked to explore the nature of love by considering different types of love based on four Greek words for love:

Storge: *affection or family love e.g. the natural affection parents have for their children.*
Eros: *romantic love.*
Philia: *friendship e.g. a common bond with those whose company you enjoy, and with whom you share common interests.*
Agape: *unconditional, self-giving love.*

Story

Joe woke up with his alarm. He hated getting up on school mornings – there was always a rush. He threw on his clothes and ran downstairs to the kitchen, where his grandma was making his grandad a cup of tea. Grandad appeared shortly after him, gave his wife a kiss on the cheek, and gratefully sat down to breakfast.

Joe looked out of the window; it was raining. He hated walking to school in the rain. Grandad saw Jo looking out of the window and offered to give him a lift to school, so he didn't have to start the day wet. Joe smiled – he liked staying with his grandparents because they were always kind to him.

Monday was Joe's favourite day because he had science with his best friend, Lisa. Joe and Lisa had been friends since primary school and they always worked together in science. As they were sitting listening to the teacher talk, Joe's mind wandered to how beautiful he thought Lisa looked. He wished they could be more than just friends.

Darren, Joe's mate, asked if he could come over after school so that they could work together on their RE project about loving your neighbours. Joe said 'yes', so when school finished they walked home together. As they were about to reach Joe's grandparents' house, a little old lady in front of them tripped on the pavement and fell down. Joe and Darren looked at each other – they had a lot of work to do and they'd wanted time to play on the Wii. Stopping to help a stranger could be a major hold-up. But both of the boys felt sorry for the old lady, so they went to see if she was OK. Unfortunately, she was very distressed and it looked like she had broken her wrist. The boys called an ambulance for her and then waited with her until it had arrived.

When Joe and Darren eventually got home, they were pleased to find that grandad had made Joe's favourite dish for dinner. Joe gave his grandad a hug – good food was going to make RE homework so much better.

Preparation: Each pupil will need a copy of worksheet 2.1: *Different types of love*. If possible, project the worksheet onto the board, or copy the columns up on the board.

- Make sure pupils understand the four types of love, asking them to give an example of an expression of each type if necessary.
- Explain that you are going to read a story in which these different types of love feature. As you read the story, pupils should note down in the appropriate column every time they hear an action demonstrating this type of love.
- Once you have read the story (on page 14) ask the class to identify which characters showed which types of love.
  - Which relationships showed more than one type of love?

Languages of love
20 minutes - Small group activity

Preparation: Each small group will need a copy of worksheet 2.2: *Five love languages.*[10]

- Give each group a copy of worksheet 2.2: *Five love languages,* and ask pupils to think of 3–5 examples of how each 'love language' could be shown.
- Ask each group to put the five love languages in order of importance.
  - Which love language could you live without?
- Feedback to the class.
- Use the four types of love from the first activity (worksheet 2.1) to write a list of the different human relationships which involve love of some sort. Which love languages are appropriate for these relationships? Would any of them be inappropriate?

Love is...
15 minutes - Small group activity

Preparation: Each small group will need a copy of worksheet 2.4: *1 Corinthians 13: blank double bubble.*

- Ask each small group to write a list of character 'ingredients' one might need to build a good relationship. Write the following unfinished sentences on the board to help them:
  'If you love someone you will be…'
  'If you love someone you will not be…'
- Once they have done this, project worksheet 2.3: *1 Corinthians 13: double bubble* onto the board.

---

10. Gary Chapman, *The Five Love Languages: How to Express Heartfelt Commitment to your Mate* (Moody Publishers, 2004).

- If pupils are not familiar with the passage, read 1 Corinthians 13 out to the class before continuing with the exercise. It may be useful for each group to have a bible open at the passage.
- Give each small group a copy of worksheet 2.4: *1 Corinthians 13: blank double bubble*. Ask pupils to fill it in using their character ingredients, showing which characteristics their list shares with Paul and which it does not.
- Once they have done this, ask pupils to pick 1–3 characteristics from their list, and think of an occasion when it would be difficult to put characteristics into practice.
- Feedback to the class:
    - What 'ingredients' on your list are different to those mentioned by Paul?
    - Do the rest of the class think these are important? Why/why not?
    - Are there any things on Paul's list with which you do not agree? Why/why not?

Extension questions

- Write the following statement on the board and ask pupils whether or not they agree with it:
    'It is more important to fancy the person you date than to be friends with them.'

Plenary: Firm foundations
10 minutes - Individual activity

Preparation: Each pupil will need a copy of worksheet 2.5: *Firm foundations.*

- Give each pupil a worksheet. Ask them to fill in the foundation blocks with characteristics that they feel are important in a good relationship.
- Once they have done this, ask them to add around the house characteristics that might damage or even destroy a relationship.
- Finally, ask them to answer the 'reflection questions' on the sheet.

Worksheet 2.1: *Different types of love*

Philia: Love for your friends	Eros: Romantic or erotic love	Agape: Spiritual love for all people	Storge: Love for your family

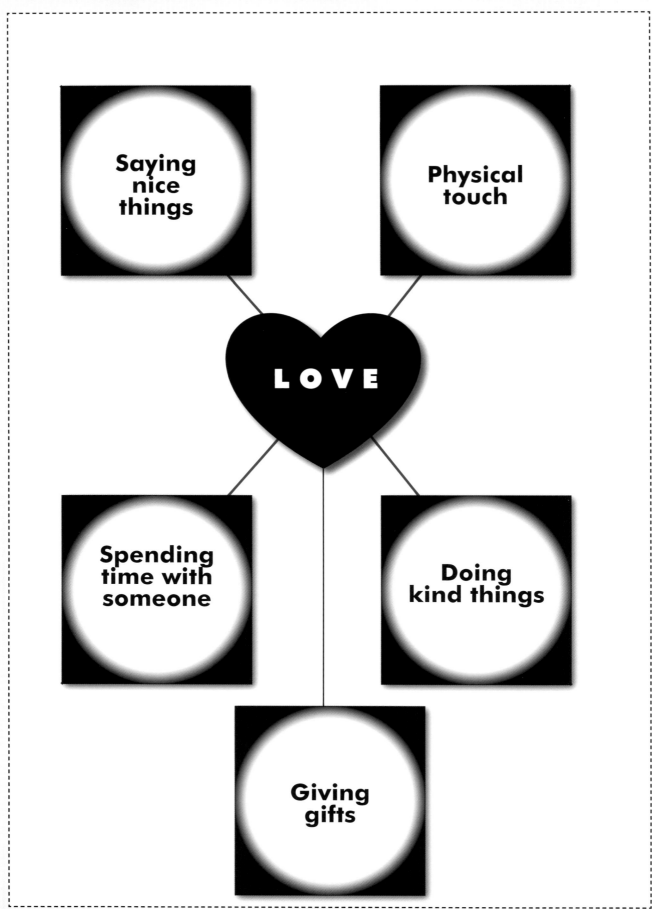

11. Gary Chapman, *The Five Love Languages: How to Express Heartfelt Commitment to your Mate* (Moody Publishers, 2004).

Worksheet 2.3: 1 Corinthians 13: double bubble

Which of your characteristics are the same as Paul's? Write the ones that are the same in the middle and the ones that are different on the outside e.g.

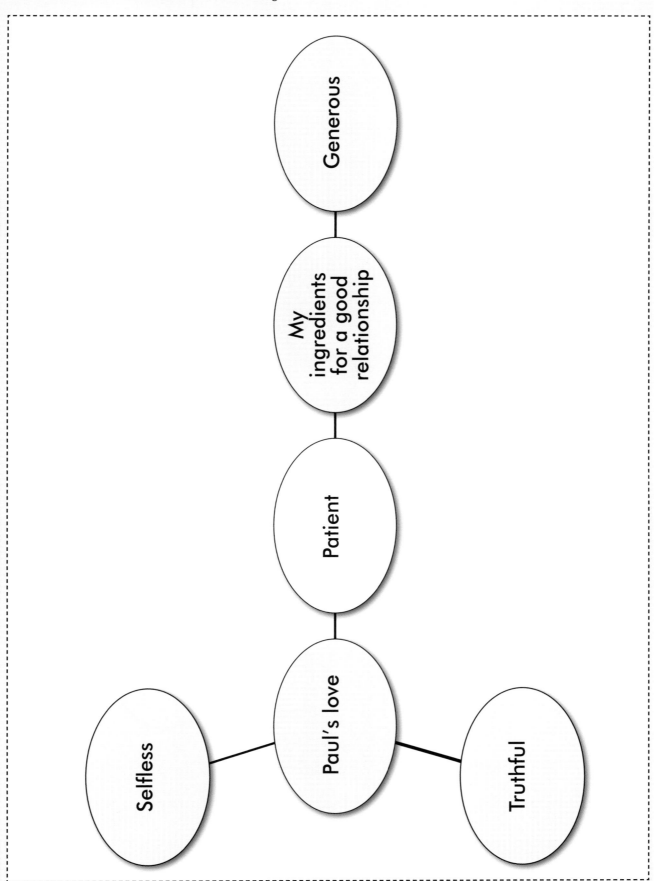

Worksheet 2.4: 1 Corinthians 13: *blank double bubble*

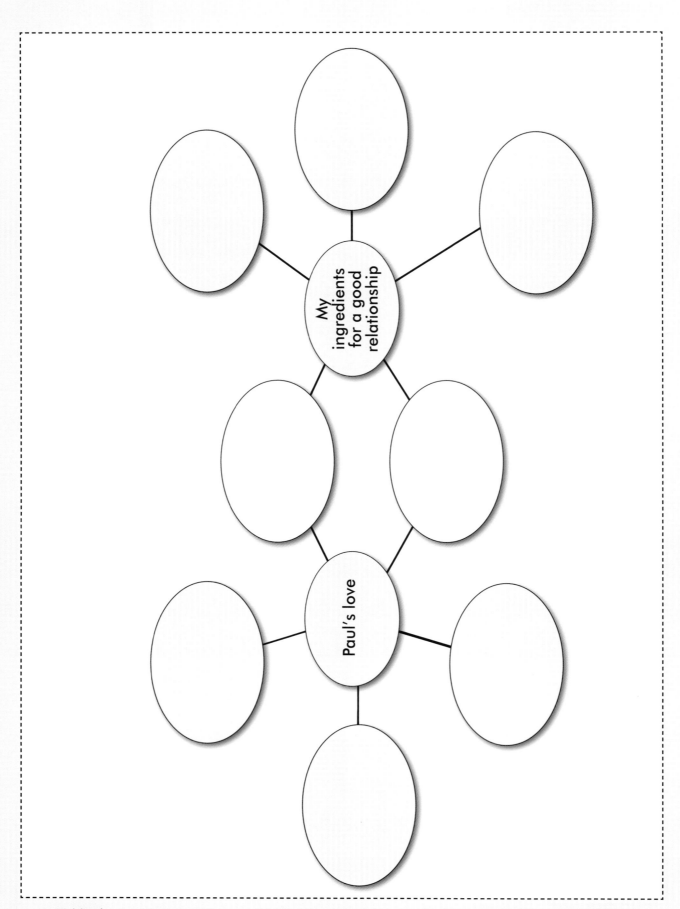

My ingredients for a good relationship

Paul's love

Worksheet 2.5: *Firm foundations*

- Which 'foundation' characteristics do you already have?
- Which 'foundation' characteristics would you like to grow in yourself?
- Why do you think these are important?

Firm foundations

Lesson 3

In this lesson pupils will think about the benefits and difficulties of marriage. They will reflect on the impact marriage has on the individual, the couple, the family and the wider community. They will also consider the spiritual aspects of marriage and how Christians believe it can draw a person closer to God. Pupils will participate in a debate comparing marriage to co-habitation. Finally, they will consider the importance of commitment in maintaining relationships.

Learning Objectives
- Reflect on how love and commitment in marriage can benefit the individual and the community, based on a Christian perspective.
- Consider the advantages and disadvantages of co-habitation versus marriage.

Learning Outcomes
- I can explain why Christians believe marriage can be a good thing for the people involved and the community of which they are part.
- I can give reasons why some people decide to co-habit, whilst others decide to get married.

Lesson Activities and Resources
- Introduction (10 minutes)
  - Film clip of wedding (not provided)
- The marvel of marriage (20 minutes)
  - Worksheet 3.1: *Marriage mind map*
  - Worksheet 3.2: *Marvel of marriage*
- The marriage debate (20 minutes)
  - Worksheet 3.3: *Marriage facts*
- Plenary: Commitment (10 minutes)

PSHE Curriculum
This lesson covers:

1.3.a. Understanding that relationships affect everything we do in our lives and that relationship skills have to be learnt and practised.

2.3.b. Pupils should be able to use the social skill of negotiation within relationships, recognising their rights and responsibilities and that their actions have consequences.

3.i. The study of personal wellbeing should include the features of positive and stable relationships, how to deal with a breakdown in a relationship and the effects of loss and bereavement.

3.k. The study of personal wellbeing should include the nature and importance of marriage and of stable relationships for family life and bringing up children.

Introduction
10 minutes - Whole class activity

- Show a film clip of a wedding, e.g. *My Big Fat Greek Wedding* (2002), Scene 17; *Fiddler on the Roof* (1971).
- Ask pupils to identify parts of the marriage service which show the importance of the following groups in the marriage:
  - The couple
  - The families of the couple
  - The wider community
  - God/a faith or belief
- Write the following statement on the board:
  > 'A wedding lasts a day; marriage lasts a lifetime.'
  - In what ways do you think the wedding day is important for a marriage?

The marvel of marriage
20 minutes - Small group activity

Preparation: Each small group will need a copy of worksheet 3.1: *Marriage mind map.*

- Give each small, mixed-ability group a copy of worksheet 3.1: *Marriage mind map.*
- Project worksheet 3.2: *Marvel of marriage* statements onto the board.
  Each statement says something about the significance of marriage or how marriage can enrich our relationships.
- Pupils need to read each statement and decide to which of the headings (community, family, couple, individual, God) it relates. They then write the statement's number in the corresponding section on the diagram.
  Some statements relate to more than one heading.
- Feedback to the class, starting the discussion with the following questions:
  - Are any of the ideas expressed here new to you/are there any ideas you did not fully understand?
  - Which statements do you agree/not agree with?

Extension question

- In what other ways might marriage enrich the relationships in the diagram?

The marriage debate
20 minutes - Small group/whole class activity

Preparation: Each small group will need a copy of worksheet 3.3: *Marriage facts.*

- Write the motion 'I believe that it is better to get married than to co-habit or live alone' on the board.
- Take an initial vote on who supports the motion, who opposes and who abstains.
- Divide the class into an even number of small groups: allocate half to argue in favour of marriage and half against.
- Tell each group to nominate one person to be their speaker.
- Hand out worksheet 3.3: *Marriage facts.*
- Give pupils about five minutes to formulate their ideas. If necessary, write the following questions on the board to help them plan what they are going to say:
    - What does a marriage offer that just a long-term relationship does not?
    - How does a person's decision about how to live affect their children/family/ community/faith?
- Debate the motion:
    - Ask one group to speak for a minute in favour of the motion.
    - Ask another group to speak for a minute against the motion.
    - Open the debate to the floor.
    - Conclude by asking one group to sum up the arguments for the motion and one to sum up the arguments against the motion.
- At the end, take a second vote to see which side has won.

Plenary: Commitment
10 minutes - Pairs activity

- Write the following statement on the board:
    'In Britain there is a high divorce rate
    because people marry for romance.'
- Ask pupils to write answers to the following questions in pairs:
    - Is love the same as romance?
    - Is commitment more important than romance in marriage?
    - Why do you think that marriage does not always work out?
    - Why is it hard to commit to another person regardless of what happens?

Worksheet 3.1: *Marriage mind map*

Read each statement on worksheet 3.2: *Marvel of marriage* and decide which of the following headings it relates to. Write the number of the statement in the appropriate box. Some statements may go in more than one box.
For example, statement 1 relates to both the individual, and the couple.

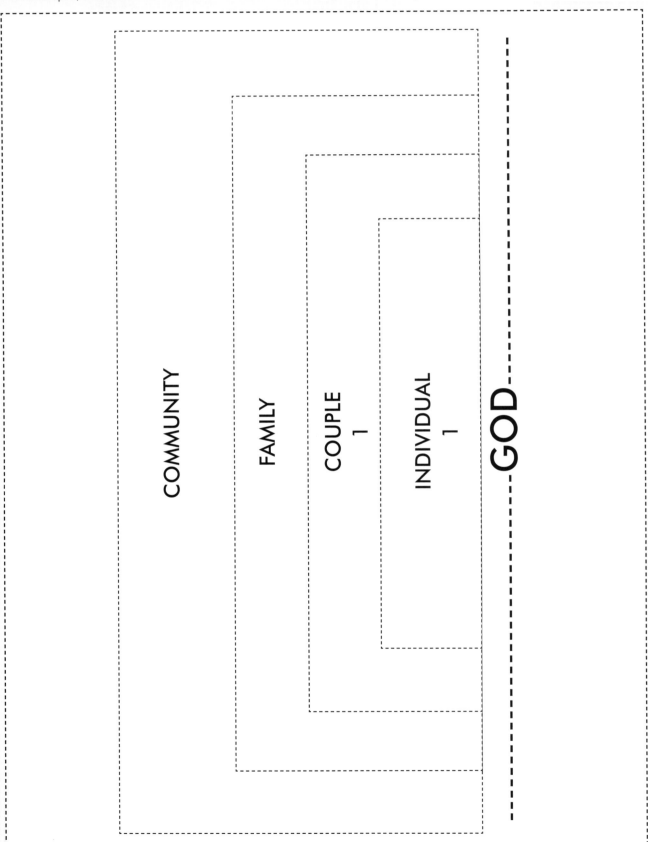

COMMUNITY

FAMILY

COUPLE
1

INDIVIDUAL
1

GOD

Worksheet 3.2: *Marvel of marriage*

1.
When people get married, they make life-long promises in front of their friends, who agree to support them. Making a public promise and asking for friends' support gives a more solid foundation, which will help the couple's relationship last.

2.
A good marriage strengthens community, by providing a secure environment for people to develop.

3.
The purpose of marriage is for man and woman to grow together in love and trust, being united with one another in heart, body and mind.
The Church of England Marriage Service

4.
Marriage is about more than just stability. It's about the risk of sharing your whole lives and wanting to be with someone so much that you give up your own freedom. You make a huge promise intended for life, without knowing whether you will be able to keep it.
Paraphrase of Rowan Williams in Mike Highton, *Difficult Gospel: The Theology of Rowan Williams,* p.145

5.
Marriage is designed to be the foundation of family life in which children are born and [looked after] and in which each member of the family, in good times and in bad, may find strength, companionship and comfort, and grow to maturity in love.
The Church of England Marriage Service

6.
Marriage can give as deep a glimpse into the heart and soul of another being as we shall ever have.
Mike Mason, *The Mystery of Marriage,* p.35

7.
In marriage you choose to experience the closeness of God in the form of a relationship with another person.

8.
Marriage is about two people committing to one another through thick and thin. The security this offers gives each individual the chance to flourish, becoming more of who God made them to be.

9.
Marriage is a gift from God. Through loving one another, even when life is hard, couples learn more about God's love.

Worksheet from *Love & Sex Matters*, KS3 resources © Salisbury Diocesan Board of Education, Bristol Diocesan Board of Education & Hope's Place.

Worksheet 3.3: *Marriage facts*

Use the facts below to argue for or against marriage.

'It is estimated that the average wedding costs £20,273.'

'The Facts of Life', *The Independent* (Tuesday 16 September 2008)

'Families based on marriage are, on average, healthier, wealthier and more stable than other family forms.'

Civitas, *Does Marriage Matter*, pp.2–3.

'In 2004/2005, figures suggested that around 45% of marriages end in divorce.'

Claire Truscott, 'Nearly Half of Marriages End in Divorce', *Guardian* (Thursday 27 March 2008)

'Couples who live together, on average, report lower quality relationships than married couples – with cohabitees reporting more conflict, more violence, and lower levels of satisfaction and commitment.'

Civitas, *Does Marriage Matter*, p.5.

'There are many legal benefits to being married. For example, if you have children together you are both legally responsible for the child. It is also assumed that you both own everything, so if your spouse dies you can inherit their property and money without having to pay tax. Co-habiting couples do not have these benefits.'

Definition
Cohabitation: living with a partner as 'husband and wife', but without legally being married.

Worksheet from *Love & Sex Matters*, KS3 resources © Salisbury Diocesan Board of Education, Bristol Diocesan Board of Education & Hope's Place.

Lesson 4 Great expectations?

In this lesson pupils reflect on the significance and meaning of the act of sexual intercourse. They will consider what makes dating relationships special and why it is important to be careful with whom you make yourself open and vulnerable. Pupils will think about what messages are given about sex and how these contribute to sexual activity. They will learn about the emotional and spiritual aspects of sex based on the some of the opinions held within different world religions.

Learning Objectives
- Reflect on the meaning and significance of sex and what causes people to become sexually active.
- Reflect on the understanding of the significance and meaning of sex in different world religions.

Learning Outcomes
- I can suggest reasons why sex can be a meaningful and loving act.
- I can suggest reasons why some young people become sexually active early.
- I can describe what Christianity and other world religions believe to be significant about sex.

Lesson Activities and Resources
- Introduction: Sharing me (10 minutes)
  - A box with lid, or a picture of a box with a lid.
- Sex is significant because... (20 minutes)
- Sex and religion (20 minutes)
  - Worksheet 4.1a/4.1b: *Sex and religion*
  - Worksheet 4.2: *Who thinks...?*
- Plenary (10 minutes)
  - Worksheet 4.3: *Sex shows that...*
- Extra activity: Sex is for... (20 minutes)
  - Worksheet 4.4: *Sex is for...*

PSHE Curriculum
This lesson covers:
2.1.a. Pupils should be able to reflect critically on their own and others' values.
2.2.a. Use knowledge and understanding to make informed choices about safety, health and wellbeing.
3.d. The study of personal wellbeing should include sexual activity, human reproduction, contraception, pregnancy, and sexually transmitted infections and HIV and how high-risk behaviours affect the health and wellbeing of individuals, families and communities.

Introduction - Sharing me
10 minutes - Whole class activity

- Use either a real box (with a lid), or a picture of a box on the board. This box represents 'me'.
- The outside of the box is what everyone sees. Ask pupils to suggest which parts of 'me' everyone sees. (Think about both physical traits and personal characteristics.) Write these on the outside of the box, or around the outside of the picture of the box.
  - Are these things that you choose to share with people, or that you have no control over sharing with them?
  - If you choose, why do you choose to show these things? If you do not choose, how do you feel about everyone seeing these things?
- The inside of the box contains the things that you hide from everyone. Ask pupils to suggest what these things inside the box are. (Again, these can be both physical traits and personal characteristics.) Write these on the inside of the lid, or by the picture of the box.
  - Which people do you allow to see these things? Why do you allow these people and not others?
- When people date, they often want to share some or all of what is 'in the box' with their partner.
  - Why do you think this is?
  - What does it say about the importance of romantic relationships?
  - What is the purpose of not sharing what's in the box with everyone?
  - How do you judge when it is right to share things in the box with someone?
  - How do you think you would feel about breaking up with someone if you had shared a lot of what is 'in the box' with them?
  - How do you think you would feel if someone took something from the box you did not want them to have?

Sex is significant because...
20 minutes - Small group activity

- If possible, show a clip of young people giving their opinions about sex. There are several clips on Truetube:
  - *The Debate: No Love, No Sex* http://www.truetube.co.uk/media. php?do=detail&mediaid=14
  - *Vox Pops on Sex and Love* http://www.truetube.co.uk/media.php?do=detail&mediaid=17
- Using the clip to give them ideas, give pupils 3 minutes to come up with a list of as many reasons as possible why young people might decide to become sexually active.
- Once they have done this, ask each group to put their reasons on a scale from 'good reasons for having sex' to 'bad reasons for having sex'.

- Feedback to the class. Start discussion with the following questions:
  - How do the media and advertising influence when young people decide to have sex? Do you think this is a good influence?
  - How important is peer pressure in a young person's decision to become sexually active? Is this a good reason to start having sex?
  - Think back to the 'box'. Do you think that your sexuality and sex life are on the inside or the outside of the box? Why?

Sex and religion
20 minutes - Small group activity

Preparation: There are two versions of worksheet 4.1: *Sex and religion*. Version 4.1b is a simpler version. Select the version that is most appropriate for your class. Each small group will need a copy of cards on worksheet 4.1a/4.1b: *Sex and religion*.
Each pupil will need a copy of worksheet 4.2: *Who thinks…?*

- Explain that different religions have slightly different understandings of why sex is important.
- Project your chosen version of worksheet 4.1: *Sex and religion* onto the board.
- Give each pupil a copy of worksheet 4.2 *Who thinks…?*. Ask pupils to fill it in individually, using the information on the board.
- Now get pupils into small groups and give each group a set of the 9 *Sex and religion* cards.
- Ask each group to arrange their cards to make a 'Diamond Nine' shape (i.e. in rows of 1 – 2 – 3 – 2 – 1), with the opinion they like/agree with most at the top and the one they like least at the bottom. *(Use the questions on the bottom of the 'Who thinks…?' sheet to aid discussion if necessary.)*
- Feedback to the class.
  - Which opinions were the most difficult to place? Why?
  - Do you think that the different religions have important messages about sex, even for people who do not belong to those religions? Why/why not?

Extension questions

- To what extent do you think that sex ties you to someone?
- Would it be OK just to walk away after having sex with someone? Why/why not?

Plenary
10 minutes - Small group and class activity

Preparation: Each small group will need a copy of worksheet 4.3: *Sex shows that…*

- Give each small mixed-ability group a copy of worksheet 4.3: *Sex shows that...* to fill in.
- Feedback to the class, asking groups to share their completed sentence: 'Sex shows that...'
- Put one or more of these quotes up on the board for discussion:

    'Sexual love ... prompts between human beings things that are like prayer; a noticing, a paying attention, a respecting of the holiness of the other person, a longing to communicate at deeper levels of being.'

    paraphrase of Alan Ecclestone

    '"God thought that it was good." Part of the joy of the commitment of marriage is that it offers a safe space to enjoy having fun with one another's bodies.'

    '"To give and receive sexually is an outward sign of an inward grace;" this is my body – my life given for you; "the breaking open of self for the other."'

    Philip Sheldrake

- What features of sex make it a spiritual act according to the writers?
- Has your view of sex changed today?
- Have you learnt something new?

Extra activity: Sex is for...
20 minutes - Small group activity

This activity is taken from *Love and Sex Matters*, Key Stage 2, Lesson 6. It is designed to help pupils think about who and what sex is for.

Preparation: Each small group will need both pages of worksheet 4.4: *Sex is for...*

- Give each small group a copy of worksheet 4.4: *Sex is for...*
- Ask pupils to cut out the statements for the 'What is sex for?' section, adding their own ideas into the blank cards if they want, then sort them into the 'true' and 'false' columns (if necessary, add a 'not sure' column).
- They should then do the same thing for the 'Who is sex for?' section.
- Feedback to the group:
    - Which statements do pupils agree/disagree with?
    - Which perspectives or ideas are new to them?

Extension question

- As a group, make up your own statement summarising what you think sex is for.

Worksheet 4.1a: *Sex and religion*

Here is what people from different religions might say about the importance of sex…

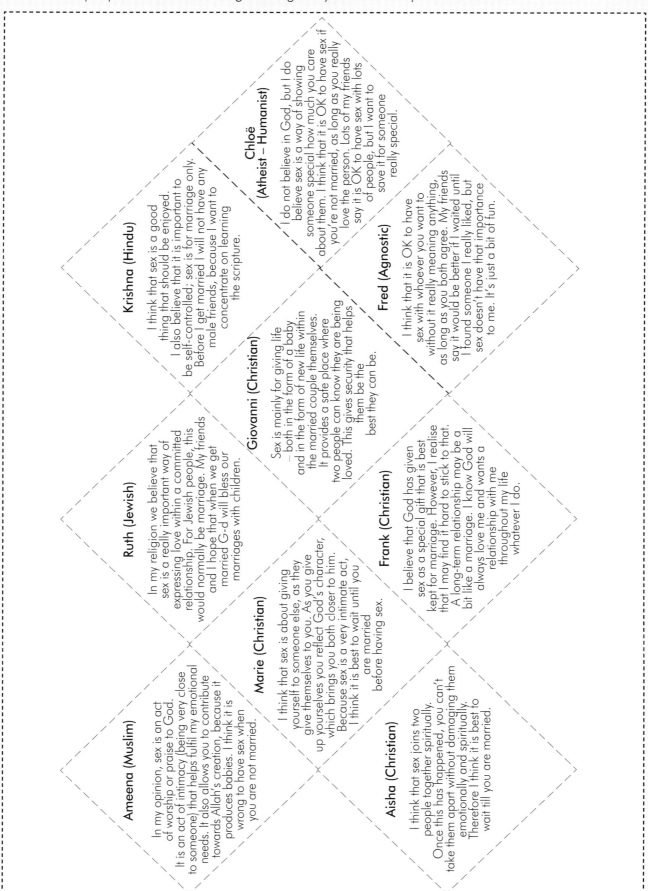

Chloë (Atheist – Humanist)

I do not believe in God, but I do believe sex is a way of showing someone special how much you care about them. I think that it is OK to have sex if you're not married, as long as you really love the person. Lots of my friends say it is OK to have sex with lots of people, but I want to save it for someone really special.

Krishna (Hindu)

I think that sex is a good thing that should be enjoyed. I also believe that it is important to be self-controlled; sex is for marriage only. Before I get married I will not have any male friends, because I want to concentrate on learning the scripture.

Fred (Agnostic)

I think that it is OK to have sex with whoever you want to without it really meaning anything, as long as you both agree. My friends say it would be better if I waited until I found someone I really liked, but sex doesn't have that importance to me. It's just a bit of fun.

Giovanni (Christian)

Sex is mainly for giving life – both in the form of a baby and in the form of new life within the married couple themselves. It provides a safe place where two people can know they are being loved. This gives security that helps them be the best they can be.

Ruth (Jewish)

In my religion we believe that sex is a really important way of expressing love within a committed relationship. For Jewish people, this would normally be marriage. My friends and I hope that when we get married G-d will bless our marriages with children.

Frank (Christian)

I believe that God has given sex as a special gift that is best kept for marriage. However, I realise that I may find it hard to stick to that. A long-term relationship may be a bit like a marriage. I know God will always love me and wants a relationship with me throughout my life whatever I do.

Marie (Christian)

I think that sex is about giving yourself to someone else, as they give themselves to you. As you give up yourselves you reflect God's character, which brings you both closer to him. Because sex is a very intimate act, I think it is best to wait until you are married before having sex.

Ameena (Muslim)

In my opinion, sex is an act of worship or praise to God. It is an act of intimacy (being very close to someone) that helps fulfil my emotional needs. It also allows you to contribute towards Allah's creation, because it produces babies. I think it is wrong to have sex when you are not married.

Aisha (Christian)

I think that sex joins two people together spiritually. Once this has happened, you can't take them apart without damaging them emotionally and spiritually. Therefore I think it is best to wait till you are married.

Worksheet 4.1b: *Sex and religion*

Here is what people from different religions might say about the importance of sex…

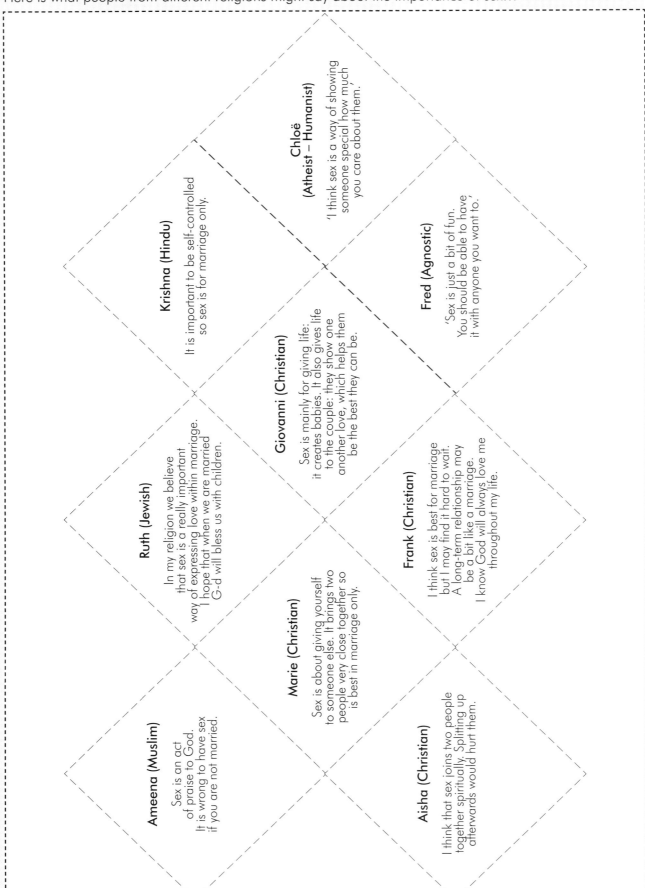

Krishna (Hindu)

It is important to be self-controlled so sex is for marriage only.

Chloë (Atheist – Humanist)

'I think sex is a way of showing someone special how much you care about them.'

Ruth (Jewish)

In my religion we believe that sex is a really important way of expressing love within marriage. I hope that when we are married G-d will bless us with children.

Giovanni (Christian)

Sex is mainly for giving life: it creates babies. It also gives life to the couple: they show one another love, which helps them be the best they can be.

Fred (Agnostic)

'Sex is just a bit of fun. You should be able to have it with anyone you want to.'

Marie (Christian)

Sex is about giving yourself to someone else. It brings two people very close together so is best in marriage only.

Frank (Christian)

I think sex is best for marriage but I may find it hard to wait. A long-term relationship may be a bit like a marriage. I know God will always love me throughout my life.

Ameena (Muslim)

Sex is an act of praise to God. It is wrong to have sex if you are not married.

Aisha (Christian)

I think that sex joins two people together spiritually. Splitting up afterwards would hurt them.

Worksheet 4.2: Who thinks...?

Use worksheet 4.1: *Sex and religion* to fill in the boxes below. Put a tick if the character agrees with the statement and a cross if they disagree. If you are unsure what someone thinks, put a question mark.

	Ameena	Ruth	Krishna	Marie	Giovanni	Chloë	Aisha	Frank	Fred
Sex is for marriage only									
You can have sex whenever you want to									
Having babies is an important part of sex									
Sex draws you closer to God									
Sex draws you closer to your partner									
Sex is a good thing									
You don't have to be married to have sex									

- Which ideas do you like or agree with? Which ones do you dislike or disagree with?

- Why?

- Are all these ideas different from the attitude of the media/Western society to sex? If some are different, in what ways are they different?

Worksheet from *Love & Sex Matters*, KS3 resources © Salisbury Diocesan Board of Education, Bristol Diocesan Board of Education & Hope's Place.

Worksheet 4.3: *Sex shows that...*

The list below states possible things that sex might symbolise. Tick 2 or 3 with which you agree. Can you add some more things it might symbolise to the bottom of the list?

- I am popular ☐

- Someone loves me ☐

- I love someone else ☐

- Nothing – it is just a bit of fun ☐

- I want to have children ☐

- I have a close relationship with my boyfriend/girlfriend ☐

- I am in spiritual union with another person ☐

- I am grown up ☐

- I am cool ☐

- I am attractive ☐

- I have biological needs to reproduce ☐

- I have made a commitment to my husband/wife ☐

- ....

- ....

- ....

- ....

- ....

- ....

- Complete the sentence: Sex shows that....

Worksheet from *Love & Sex Matters*, KS3 resources © Salisbury Diocesan Board of Education, Bristol Diocesan Board of Education & Hope's Place.

Worksheet 4.4: *Sex is for...*
What is sex for?

Making children	**Feeling loved**
Growing closer to someone emotionally	**Showing someone you love them**
Growing closer to someone spiritually	**Having fun**
Growing closer to God	**Making me happy**
Showing someone you are committed to them	**Making the other person happy**

Who is sex for?

Someone special	**Children**
Anyone	**Married people**
Grown ups	**Unmarried people**
Teenagers	

Worksheet 4.4: *Sex is for... (cont)*

What is sex for?

True	False

Who is sex for?

True	False

Lesson 5 Contraception

During this session, pupils will learn some of the facts about contraception, as well as reflecting on the ethical questions associated with it. Pupils will then learn about the different types of contraception available and how they work. The perspectives of Christianity and other world religions on contraception will also be discussed.

It will help if you are able to have a box of contraceptive devices available for demonstration.

Learning Objectives
- Discuss the facts about contraception.
- Reflect on the ethics of contraception.

Learning Outcomes
- I can name 3–5 types of contraception and explain how they work.
- I can explain what Christianity and other world religions think about contraception.

Lesson Activities and Resources
- Introduction: Mythical contraception (10 minutes)
- Contraception – What is there? (25 minutes)
    - Worksheet 5.1: *Contraception fact cards*
    - Worksheet 5.2: *Contraception facts table*
    - Box of contraceptive devices (optional)
    - Worksheet 5.3: *Completed contraception table*
- Contraception – Ethics (20 minutes)
    - Worksheet 5.4a/5.4b: *Contraception ethics cards*
    - Worksheet 5.5: *Contraception ethics table*
- Plenary: Discussion (5 minutes)

PSHE Curriculum
This lesson covers:
2.1.a. Pupils should be able to reflect critically on their own and others' values.
2.2.a. Pupils should be able to use knowledge and understanding to make informed choices about safety, health and wellbeing.
3.d. The study of personal wellbeing should include sexual activity, human reproduction, contraception, pregnancy, and sexually transmitted infections and HIV and how high-risk behaviours affect the health and wellbeing of individuals, families and communities.

Introduction - Mythical contraception
10 minutes - Whole class activity

- Put a 'TRUE' sign on one wall of the room, a 'FALSE' sign on the opposite wall, and an 'UNSURE' sign on a table in the middle of the room.
- Read out the following statements and ask pupils to move to the sign that shows what they think of the statement. After each statement, give the correct answer.

Contraception statements	
1. If a woman stands up immediately after she has had sex, she will not get pregnant – **FALSE**	5. Using contraception 100% guarantees a woman will not get pregnant – **FALSE**
2. It is possible for a woman to get pregnant the first time she has sex – **TRUE**	6. A woman can become pregnant before she has started her periods – **TRUE**
3. If a woman has sex in water, she will not get pregnant – **FALSE**	7. Since a woman is the one who will get pregnant, contraception is her responsibility, not the man's – **FALSE**
4. A woman can get pregnant when she is having her period – **TRUE**	8. A woman cannot get pregnant while she is breast-feeding – **FALSE**

Contraception – what is there?
25 minutes - Pairs activity and whole class activity

Part 1

Preparation: Worksheet 5.1: *Contraception fact cards* includes facts about eight types of contraception. You may wish to vary the number of contraceptive types given to each group depending on ability, but if you do this, make sure that every contraceptive type is represented at least once in the class.

Each pair will need a copy of worksheet 5.1: *Contraception fact cards,* and a copy of worksheet 5.2: *Contraception facts table.*

It is useful to have a box of contraceptives to show the class when discussing the table.

- Hand out worksheet 5.1: *Contraception fact cards* and worksheet 5.2: *Contraception facts table* to each pair and ask them to match up the type of contraception with the facts about it.
- Worksheet 5.3: *Completed contraception table* shows the correct answers.
- Feedback to the group, clarifying any mistakes and showing the different contraception types.

Part 2

Preparation: It will help to have a list of the types of contraception on the board for this discussion.

- Explain that contraception is only effective if it is used properly. Statistics from the Centre for Young Women's Health, Boston, show that, in reality, the way contraception is used – 'typical usage' – means it has much lower success rates.[12]
- As a whole class, rank the types of contraception from 'most effective with typical usage' to 'least effective with typical usage'.
- Once they have done this, compare their predictions with the statistics below:
  - Abstinence – 100% (as long as you actually don't have sex!)
  - Implant – 99%
  - The Coil – 99%
  - Combined pill – 95%
  - 'Morning after' pill – 75–88%
  - Condoms – 86%
  - Cap – 82%
  - Natural family planning – 76%
- Feedback and discussion
  - Which of these surprise you?
  - Do you think abstinence is a viable form of birth control? Why/why not?
- Explain that chances of becoming pregnant can be minimised by using two forms of contraception, such as the condom and the pill.

Contraception – Ethics
20 minutes - Small group activity

This may be an issue covered in GCSE RE, in which case you may want to miss out this activity.

Preparation: There are two versions of worksheet 5.4: *Contraception ethics cards*. 5.4b is a shorter and simpler version. Each group will need a copy of worksheet 5.4a/5.4b: *Contraception ethics cards* and worksheet 5.5: *Contraception ethics table*. It may be useful to have worksheet 5.3: *Completed contraception table* projected onto the board.

- Give each group a copy of worksheet 5.4a/5.4b: *Contraception ethics cards* and worksheet 5.4: *Contraception ethics table*. Ask pupils to fill in the table showing which types of contraception they think each person would be happy to use/would not use and why.
- Feedback to the class.
  - With which opinions do you agree most and why?

Plenary: Discussion
5 minutes - Whole class activity

- Some people of faith would say: 'God has given sex so we can have children. So contraception is wrong.' Do you agree? Why/why not?
- Do you think it is important to be aware of the possibility of becoming pregnant when you decide to have sex with someone?

12. See http://www.youngwomenshealth.org/summarychart.html [accessed online 18 January 2010]

Worksheet 5.1: Contraception fact cards

What is it?

- An emergency contraceptive pill.
- A thin, flexible tube that is put into the arm by a trained health professional and slowly releases the hormone progestogen.
- A tablet containing the hormones oestrogen and progestogen.
- A small T-shaped plastic and copper device that is inserted into the womb by a specially trained health professional.
- A dome made of latex or silicone that is inserted into the vagina.
- A protective layer that covers either the penis (for men) or the inside of the vagina (for women).
- Using a woman's 'body clock' to judge when it is 'safe' to have sex.
- Not having sex.

How does it work?

- It stops sperm surviving in the cervix, womb or fallopian tubes, preventing fertilisation or a fertilised egg from implanting in the womb.
- It contains hormones that change the lining of the womb so a fertilised egg cannot embed in it.
- It stops sperm entering the womb so the egg cannot be fertilised.
- It stops sperm entering the womb so the egg cannot be fertilised.
- It stops a woman ovulating, meaning there is no egg to be fertilised.
- It stops a woman ovulating, meaning there is no egg to be fertilised.
- Don't have sex.
- The menstrual cycle is used to plot when a woman is fertile and when not, so she only has sex when her body is less likely to conceive.

How practical is it?

- It has to be taken every day.
- A woman is not able to have sex for around two weeks every month.
- A woman has to have a small operation under local anaesthetic. Once it is in, it works for up to 3 years.
- It has to be put on once the penis is erect (i.e. you have to stop during sex).
- It has to be carefully inserted just before or during sex.
- A woman is guaranteed not to become pregnant, but only for as long as she does not have sex.
- A woman has to take it within 72 hours of having sex, at most.
- It has to be inserted by the doctor and can cause bleeding and heavy periods.

Worksheet 5.2: *Contraception facts table*

Use the cards from worksheet 5.1 to fill in the table below.

Name	What is it?	How does it work?	Who uses it?	How practical is it?
Condom			Man or woman	
Combined pill			Woman	
Cap			Woman	
Natural family planning			Woman	
'Morning-after' pill			Woman	
Abstinence			Man or woman	
The coil			Woman	
Implant			Woman	

Worksheet 5.3: *Completed contraception table*

Name	What is it?	How does it work?	Who uses it?	How practical is it?
Condom	A protective layer that covers either the penis (for men) or the inside of the vagina (for women).	It stops sperm entering the womb so the egg cannot be fertilised.	Man or woman	It has to be put on once the penis is erect (i.e. you have to stop during sex).
Combined pill	A tablet containing the hormones oestrogen and progestogen.	It stops a woman ovulating, meaning there is no egg to be fertilised.	Woman	It has to be taken every day.
Cap	A dome made of latex or silicone that is inserted into the vagina.	It stops sperm entering the womb so the egg cannot be fertilised.	Woman	It has to be carefully inserted just before or during sex.
Natural family planning	Using a woman's 'body clock' to judge when it is 'safe' to have sex.	The menstrual cycle is used to plot when a woman is fertile and when not, so she only has sex when her body is less likely to conceive.	Woman	A woman is not able to have sex for around two weeks every month.
'Morning-after' pill	An emergency contraceptive pill.	It contains hormones that change the lining of the womb so a fertilised egg cannot embed in it.	Woman	A woman has to take it within 72 hours of having sex, at most.
Abstinence	Not having sex.	Don't have sex.	Man or woman	A woman is guaranteed not to become pregnant, but only for as long as she does not have sex.
The coil	A small T-shaped plastic and copper device that is inserted into a woman's womb by a specially trained health professional.	It stops sperm surviving in the cervix, womb or fallopian tubes, preventing fertilisation or a fertilised egg from implanting in the womb.	Woman	It has to be inserted by the doctor and can cause bleeding and heavy periods.
Implant	A thin, flexible tube that is put into a woman's arm by a trained health professional and slowly releases the hormone progestogen.	It stops a woman ovulating, meaning there is no egg to be fertilised.	Woman	A woman has to have a small operation under local anaesthetic. Once it is in, it works for up to 3 years.

Worksheet 5.4a: *Contraception ethics cards*

Marie (Christian)
Because I think that sex is a way of showing someone you love them by giving yourself to them, I think it is OK to use contraception. You do not have to want to conceive every time you have sex. However, because I believe that life begins at fertilisation, I do not think it is OK to use contraception that works after fertilisation.

Giovanni (Christian - Catholic)
I believe in abstinence (not having sex) before marriage. Once you are married, I believe that having babies is an important part of sex so I do not think that you should use artificial forms of contraception. I believe that they go against God's purpose for sex and limit the significance of it being part of a married relationship.

Hari (Buddhist)
My religion does not say that having children is a religious duty so I think it is fine to use contraception. Having said that, I think that at the moment of fertilisation a life has come into existence and so it is wrong to do anything to destroy this.

Krishna (Hindu)
When people are not married I believe it is best to practice self-control and not have sex, so no contraception would be required. My scriptures do not give exact advice on contraception but like most modern Hindus I think that in order to reduce suffering and over-population, contraception within marriage is a good idea.

Ameena (Muslim)
I believe that sex is for marriage only, so how contraception is used is only important when you are married. In this case, it is OK to use contraception that prevents fertilisation, though you should not use it forever: having children is a gift from Allah.

Chloë (Atheist - Humanist)
I think that everyone should take responsibility for his/her own actions. So if I have sex, it is my job to make sure I do not get pregnant before I am ready to settle down and start a family. Contraception helps me do this. However, my personal preference would be to use something that does not interfere with my hormones.

Ruth (Jewish)
Jewish people do not always agree about contraception. Many Jewish people do not encourage contraception, unless pregnancy will make the mother ill. If contraception is used, it is better that the woman uses it to avoid the man wasting his sperm.

Jasminder (Sikh)
In my religion, there are no fixed rules about birth control. It is up to the couple to decide what sort of contraception, if any, they want to use. However, every couple should aim one day to contribute to Waheguru's (the one God's) creation.

Worksheet from Love & Sex Matters, KS3 resources © Salisbury Diocesan Board of Education, Bristol Diocesan Board of Education & Hope's Place.

Worksheet 5.4b: *Contraception ethics cards*

Marie (Christian)
I think it is OK to use contraception because sex is about more than having children. However, I believe life begins at fertilisation, so a fertilised egg should not be destroyed.

Giovanni (Christian - Catholic)
I believe in abstinence before marriage. Once you are married, having children is an important part of sex so nothing unnatural should be done to prevent this.

Hari (Buddhist)
I also believe that life begins at conception, so I would not use contraception that works after fertilisation.

Krishna (Hindu)
I think no sex before marriage is the best birth control. When I am at the right stage in life, I will have a family.

Ameena (Muslim)
I think it is OK to use contraception that stops fertilisation for a bit, as long as you plan to have children eventually.

Chloë (Atheist)
Contraception helps you take responsibility, so you do not become pregnant by mistake.

Ruth (Jewish)
I would not use contraception that stops the sperm entering the woman's body.

Jasminder (Sikh)
In my religion there are no rules about birth control, but every couple should aim one day to contribute to Waheguru's (the one God's) creation.

Worksheet 5.5: *Contraceptive ethics table*

Name	Contraception they would use	Contraception they wouldn't use
Marie		
Giovanni		
Hari		
Krishna		
Ameena		
Chloë		
Ruth		
Jasminder		

Risky choices

This lesson is about risks. Pupils will think about the health risks (STIs) involved in sleeping with someone you do not know and consider to what extent you have an obligation to the wider community to be aware of personal sexual health. They will consider things that hinder or impact on the decision-making process, with a particular focus on the prominent role drugs and alcohol play in sexual assault. Pupils will also be encouraged to think about what the term 'safer sex' means and the ways in which sex is and is not 'safe'.

Learning Objectives
- Discuss the facts about and reflect on the moral questions associated with STIs.
- Reflect on the things that hinder good decision-making and how to manage them, in particular the effects of alcohol and drugs.
- Think about what 'safer sex' means.

Learning Outcomes
- I can name 3–5 STIs and can describe how you get them.
- I can explain why using alcohol and drugs is risky.
- I can explain what 'safer sex' means.

Lesson Activities and Resources
- Introduction: The STI game (10 minutes)
  - A piece of paper for each pupil
  - Music to play
- STI facts (15 minutes)
  - Powerpoint/worksheet 6.1: *STI facts*
- When to stop? (10 minutes)
- Risky decisions (15 minutes)
- Plenary: 'Safer sex'? (10 minutes)

PSHE Curriculum
This lesson covers:
1.2.a Recognising that healthy lifestyles, and the wellbeing of self and others, depend on information and making responsible choices.

2.1.f Pupils should be able to develop self-awareness by reflecting critically on their behaviour and its impact on others.

2.2.f Pupils should be able to assess and manage the element of risk in personal choices and situations.

3.d. The study of personal wellbeing should include sexual activity, human reproduction, contraception, pregnancy, and sexually transmitted infections and HIV and how high-risk behaviours affect the health and wellbeing of individuals, families and communities.

Introduction - The STI game
10 minutes - Whole class activity

Preparation: You'll need a small piece of paper for each pupil. Mark some of the pieces of paper with an 'x', this sign is a 'booster'.
Pick two numbers between 1 and 7. These are neutral. Allocate an STI to all of the other numbers. Have some music ready to play for the game.

- As pupils come into the room, give them each one of the small pieces of paper.
- Explain that today's lesson is about taking risks.
- Ask pupils to write a number between 1 and 7 on their piece of paper.
- Explain that some numbers represent sexually transmitted infections, whilst others do not. The 'booster' symbol means this person is under the influence of alcohol and they have extra speed in the game.
- Play the STI game:

Game

This game is like Musical Bumps:
- As some music plays, pupils should move around the room.
- When the music stops, pupils should ask the person nearest to them if they want to swap numbers. If they agree, each person should write the other person's number on their own piece of paper.
- Pupils who have the 'boost' symbol are allowed to swap numbers whilst the music is playing as well.
- Repeat this process a few times.
- After a few minutes, ask pupils to return to their seats.

STI facts
15 minutes - Whole class activity

- Once the pupils have sat down, go through the numbers one by one, asking for a show of hands as to how many people have each one.
- After each show of hands, reveal what the number represents and, if it is an STI, use powerpoint/worksheet 6.1: *STI facts* to give facts about each disease. If you wish to show the class photos as well, there are many available on the internet, for example at http://herpes-coldsores.com/std/ or at http://yourstdhelp.com/herpes.html.
- Feedback:
  - When you asked someone for his/her number, did you know whether it represented an STI? What are the implications of this for sleeping around?
- Tell pupils that condoms are the only type of contraception that offers some protection against STIs, but using one does not guarantee total protection.
  Make sure pupils know where they can go to have an STI test, e.g. GP surgery, Genito-urinary medicine (GUM) clinic etc.

Extension questions

Jo hangs out with a group of lads who like partying and having one-night stands. However, last week he found out he has HIV.

- Does Jo have a moral obligation to tell potential partners that he has HIV? Why/why not?
- Does a person have a moral responsibility to find out whether they have an STI before sleeping with someone? Why/why not?

When to stop?
10 minutes - Whole class activity

- Read the story aloud to the class, pausing where indicated.
- Each time you pause, pupils should assess the risk factor of the situation and decide whether they think the character should proceed, proceed with caution or stop.
- Once they have decided, they should show their opinion by a 'thumbs up' (proceed), 'wobbling their thumbs' (proceed with caution) or 'thumbs down' (stop).
- Once a pupil has displayed a 'thumbs down', they are no longer allowed to play the game.

Story

Fifteen-year-old Amira's best friend, Hannah, is turning 16. All her friends want to go out to celebrate. The plan is to go down to the pub, have a few drinks and then maybe go to a club. Should Amira go? **Pause.**
Amira knew that all her friends would be dressed up. Her big sister said she could borrow her new mini-skirt and sparkly top. Amira wants to look good, but is a bit worried because the skirt and top look very short and tight. Should she wear them? **Pause.**
At 7.30 her friends come round to meet her and they call a taxi to take them to the pub. Should she get in it? **Pause.**
On arriving at the pub, they meet up with a group of guys. Paul – the gang leader – offers to buy them all a drink. Although Amira knows she is underage, she really wants a vodka and lemonade. She knows Paul would get her one if she asked. Should she ask for one? **Pause.**
About half an hour later, Bruno offers her another drink. Amira really likes Bruno and wants his attention. Should she say yes? **Pause.**
Bruno comes back with her order and two shots of tequila. He says they should both do a shot first. Amira doesn't really like tequila, but she does like Bruno. Should she say yes? **Pause.**

• **INFORMATION** • Tell the class that both Bruno and Paul had in fact bought Amira doubles not singles; she had not had a proper dinner because she was worried about not looking her best, so by now she is extremely drunk.

Bruno buys a few more drinks and Amira starts to think he might actually like her. Eventually, he asks her if she wants him to drop her home. She had planned to go back with her friends, but she really likes Bruno. Should she say yes? **Pause.**
Amira is too drunk to stand up properly, so Bruno says he will carry her. However, they don't go to Amira's – Bruno says he wants to pick something up from his house first. But when they get there, he says he thinks it would be better if she just stayed at his. Should she say yes? **Pause.**
Amira tries to say no, but she is too drunk to argue with Bruno. When he puts her on his bed and starts kissing her, she is too drunk to stop him. So Amira loses her virginity to Bruno.

- If all pupils have shown a 'thumbs down' before the end of the story, tell them what would have happened had they not.
- Feedback:
  - Who do you think is responsible or guilty for what happened – Bruno or Amira?
  Why?
  - How do you think drugs and alcohol affect your ability to make good decisions about sexual activity?
- Explain that experiencing a sexual assault is highly traumatic and can be hard to talk about. Specialist help is available e.g. Childline, NSPCC.
- You may also want to tell pupils that the majority of people who commit sexual assaults and date rapes know their victims, so getting drunk with your friends is not necessarily safer. (See http://rds.homeoffice.gov.uk/rds/pdfs04/r125.pdf for more information.)

Risky decisions
15 minutes - Small group activity

- Ask pupils, in small groups, to brainstorm the things that caused Amira to make risky decisions.
  - What might or could have stopped her making such risky decisions?
  - Which things help good decision-making? Why?
- Feedback:
  - What do you think are the physical risks of a sexual experience like Amira's? (e.g. STIs, pregnancy)
  - What do you think are the emotional risks?
  - How do you think Amira might have felt after what happened?

Safer sex?
10 minutes - Whole class activity

- Ask pupils what they think the term 'safer sex' means. Form a definition and write it on the board.
  - What could a person do if he/she wanted to have 'safer sex'?
  - Do these things protect a person emotionally and spiritually? What might help protect someone in this way?

Powerpoint/Worksheet 6.1: *STI facts*

Chlamydia

- Passed on through semen/vaginal fluid when you have unprotected sex.
- Very often there are no external signs of this; you have to have a test to be sure.
- If it is treated early, it is unlikely to cause infertility; however, if left it can cause infertility and other infections.
- 150% increase in the number of cases between 1998 and 2007 (based on STI diagnoses at GUM clinics in the UK). It is estimated that 10% of under-25s have this infection.

Genital herpes

- Enters body through small cracks in skin/mucous membranes, so can be passed on through any sexual contact (touch; kissing, particularly if someone has a cold sore; sex etc).
- Often no symptoms, though you may get small blisters around bottom/thighs and experience pain going to the loo.
- It can sort itself out, though likely to be painful. No link to infertility.
- 51% increase in the number of cases between 1998 and 2007 (based on STI diagnoses at GUM clinics in the UK).

Genital Warts

- Passed on during sex, but not by kissing/hugging etc.
- Often no symptoms: you may have visible warts, but these can appear any time from 3 weeks to several years after coming into contact with the virus.
- This virus may come and go without your noticing.

Gonorrhoea

- Passed on through semen/vaginal fluid when you have unprotected sex.
- Symptoms include yellowy/green discharge and pain when going to the loo.
- Can cause long-term infertility for men and women and spread to other parts of the reproductive system, causing extreme pain.

HIV

- Passed on by any contact with body fluids, including blood and breast milk.
- Initial signs may include flu-like symptoms, though many infected people will not have any signs.
- Once you have HIV there is no way of removing it from your body.
- If it is not treated properly it can cause serious long-term damage and even death.

Pubic Lice and Scabies

- Former passed on through body contact; latter passed also by bed linen/touching someone else's hands etc.
- Cause itching in infected area; brown eggs visible on pubic hair and sometimes black lice droppings in underwear.
- Do not cause long-term problems or infertility.

Syphilis

- Passed on through sexual contact.
- Early symptoms include sores where the skin came into contact with the disease and swollen glands.
- Untreated syphilis can cause deafness, blindness or death.
- 1,828% increase in the number of cases between 1998 and 2007 (based on STI diagnoses at GUM clinics in the UK).

Lesson 7 — Why wait?

In the first part of this lesson, pupils will consider the stages of maturation involved in growing up. They will consider the different speeds at which people grow up and how these could influence when an individual feels mature enough to undertake a given activity. The second part of the lesson will draw together this and the previous two lessons, as pupils consider how knowledge of the spiritual, emotional, social and physical aspects of sex and growing up can enable more informed decisions to be made about when to become sexually active.

Learning Objectives
- Understand growing up as a process that different people go through at different speeds.
- Learn what the law says about sex.
- Reflect on when someone might be ready to become sexually active, considering spiritual, emotional, physical and social aspects.

Learning Outcomes
- I can describe some of the stages of growing up.
- I can explain what the law says about sex.
- I can give someone advice on whether or not to become sexually active, based on my knowledge of the physical, spiritual and emotional aspects of sex.

Lesson Activities and Resources
- Introduction: Stages of maturity (15 minutes)
  - Worksheet 7.1: *Stages of maturity cards*
  - Worksheet 7.2: *Stages of maturity timeline*
- Consequences (5 minutes)
- Sex and the law (5 minutes)
  - Worksheet 7.3: *Sex and the law*
- Host your own chat show! (30 minutes)
  - Worksheet 7.4: *Chat show scenarios*
  - Worksheets 4.1a/4.1b: *Sex and religion* and 5.4a/5.4b: *Contraception ethics cards*
- Plenary: Advice for all (5 minutes)

PSHE Curriculum
This lesson covers:
1.4.a. Understanding that relationships affect everything we do in our lives and that relationship skills have to be learnt and practised.
2.1.a. Pupils should be able to reflect critically on their own and others' values.
2.2.a. Pupils should be able to use knowledge and understanding to make informed choices about safety, health and wellbeing.
2.2.c. Pupils should be able to assess and manage the element of risk in personal choices and situations

Introduction - Stages of maturity
15 minutes - Pairs activity

Preparation: Each pair will need a copy of worksheet 7.1: *Stages of maturity cards,* and a copy of worksheet 7.2: *Stages of maturity timeline.*

- Give each pair a copy of worksheet 7.1: *Stages of maturity cards,* and 7.2: *Stages of maturity timeline.* Explain that the statements on the cards are 'growing-up events'. Some are 'bodily changes', some are 'activities'.
- Ask pupils to show when they think these events might happen, by putting the cards by the appropriate age. (It is worth pointing out that some physical developments may happen at different times.)
- Feedback to the class, starting discussion with questions:
  - Were any cards particularly hard to place? Why?
  - What other important 'growing up' events can you think of? Where would you place these on the timeline?
  - Do you think that these events happen to everyone at the same time? Why do you think it is important to let people grow up at their own speed?
  - How do you think that the 'bodily changes' above the line relate to the 'activities' below the line, if at all?

Consequences
5 minutes - Whole class activity

- Write 'sex' in the centre of the board and around it put four headings:
  - EMOTIONAL (how would you feel)
  - SPIRITUAL (how would it affect you spiritually – think back to what was discussed two weeks ago)
  - SOCIAL (how might it affect your relationship with family/friends)
  - PHYSICAL (the effects it might have on your body)
- Give pupils three minutes to think of as many 'consequences' of having sex as they can for each category, based on the previous three lessons.

Sex and the law
5 minutes - Whole class activity

Preparation: Each pupil will need a copy of worksheet 7.3: *Sex and the law*

- Show the Truetube vox pop about Sex and the law (http://www.truetube.co.uk/media.php?do=detail&mediaid=558)
- Ask pupils to fill in worksheet 7.3: *Sex and the law* as they go along.
- Feedback, making sure everyone has the correct answers.

Host your own chat show!
30 minutes - Small group/whole class activity

Part 1
5 minutes

Preparation: Each small group will need one scenario from worksheet 7.4: *Chat show scenarios*. There are six on the sheet. Each group should also be given one ethics card from either worksheet 4.1a/4.1b: *Sex and religion* or worksheet 5.4a/5.4b: *Contraception ethics cards*.

- Put the following question on the board to help guide pupils' discussions:
  How would an awareness of the possible consequences of sex help you to make a good decision about when to become sexually active?
- Divide the class into small groups of four or five and give each group one scenario card and one ethics card.
- Ask each group to nominate one host, one character (the main person in the scenario) and one person to give a religious opinion.
  The remaining two/three people will give their own opinion.
- Give each group two minutes to read their scenario and discuss it.

Part 2
25 minutes

- Choose a group and ask their host and character to come up to the front.
- Ask the host to introduce the character and his/her situation.
- Ask the other members of this group (who are still in their seats) to give a faith-based perspective on what the character should do, followed by their own opinion.
- Open the debate up to the whole class. What do other groups think about the advice the character has been given? Do they agree? What advice would they give, considering spiritual, emotional, social and physical perspectives?
- Finally, ask the character what he/she thinks she will do in response to the advice given.
- Now do the same with a different group and scenario. It is recommended that you aim to cover 2–3 scenarios in this time.

Plenary: Advice for all
5 minutes - Pairs/whole class activity

- Ask the pupils to discuss the following question in pairs:
  - Is there any advice which is useful for all these characters in deciding whether or not to have sex?
- Feedback to whole class.

Worksheet 7.1: *Stages of maturity cards*

Place these cards along the timeline to show when you think these things might happen to you.

I can do my own washing and ironing.	Breasts start to grow.
I grow pubic hair.	I am old enough to have a girlfriend/boyfriend.
I can get a job.	My periods start.
I have my first wet dream.	I can make decisions independently of my parents.
I can go out on my own.	I am mature enough to have sex.
I can manage my own money.	I can go out without telling my parents where I am going.
I am an adult.	I can move out of my parents' house.
I can shop for and cook my own food.	I can get married.
I can stand up in public and explain what I believe.	I can babysit.

Worksheet 7.2: *Stages of maturity timeline*

Bodily changes

0 1 2 3 4 5 6 7 8 9 10 11 12 13 14 15 16 17 18 19 20 21 22 23 24 25

Activities

Worksheet 7.3: *Sex and the law*

As an adult, legally I could have sex with...

☐ **A 15-year-old**

☐ **My parent**

☐ **A person of the same sex**

☐ **My sister**

☐ **A porcupine**

☐ **My step-brother**

☐ **A stranger**

☐ **A person against their will**

☐ **My cousin**

☐ **A person with disabilities**

Worksheet 7.3: *Sex and the law*

Worksheet 7.4: *Chat show scenarios*

Scenario 1

My name is Marika and I was married, but my husband ran off with another woman. Now I have met a man at the garage where my car was being mended. We've been out a few times and want to take it to the next level. It's only two months since my marriage ended and I have two teenagers – Seth and Marie. Would it be OK for me to have sex?

Scenario 2

I'm Muzoora and I'm sixteen. I have been going out with my fifteen-year-old girlfriend for six months now and I think I love her, though I am not sure if she feels the same about me. If we have sex it might make our relationship better. What should I do?

Scenario 3

I'm Gloria and I'm thirteen. I met this guy Jed last week at a party and he's really cute! My friends keep telling me that the way to get a boyfriend is to have sex with him. I don't want to be uncool, but I'm not sure I'm ready. What should I do?

Scenario 4

I'm Danika, I'm twenty-five, a Catholic, and I've been married to Mark for two years now. Last year I was diagnosed with cancer so am undergoing chemotherapy at the moment. If I were to become pregnant, I would have to stop the treatment because it would most probably kill the child. Should I have sex?

Scenario 5

I'm Monty, I'm seventeen, and I've been with my girlfriend, Tina, for a while now. I really like her – in fact I think I would like to marry her one day – but I am not sure that I'm ready for a family. She really wants one though… We haven't had sex yet, but I think we both want to. What should I do?

Scenario 6

I'm Narinder and I am getting married in a month. Last week, my fiancé found out that he is HIV positive. We haven't had sex yet, because I am a strict Muslim. Should I have sex once we are married?

Summary activities

These are activities relating to the course, which aim to encourage pupils' spiritual development. They aim to summarise the course, allowing pupils to reflect on what they have learnt and its application to their lives. Here, the focus is on the following questions:

- How can sex be life-giving?
- How can sex be abusive?
- How could I change my attitude/approach in order that I might be more life-giving?

Note to teachers

If it is more appropriate for your class, you can broaden the discussion to 'relationships' rather than focusing on sex.

Teachers are reminded that this may be a sensitive area for some and so should undertake the activities with due care and consideration.

It is important to remember that, whether you are aware of it or not, some pupils may have had very negative experiences of sex or sexual encounters, which could make it hard for them to undertake this exercise. Depending on pupils' backgrounds, it may or may not be appropriate to explain briefly where help is available for those who have suffered sexual abuse.

Introduction
Pairs activity

- Write the following quote up on the board:
  'When power meets power, conflict erupts. When power meets vulnerability, oppression follows. When vulnerability meets vulnerability, intimacy blooms.'
  Paraphrase of Richard G. Malloy, SJ, 'Just Sex? Giving Young Adults What They Truly Want', *Busted Halo* 17/01/08.
- Ask pupils, in pairs, to see if they can work out what the quote means and write a few sentences explaining how they understand it.
- Feedback to the group, writing some of the responses on the board.
  - Do you agree with the statement? Why/why not?

Card sorting
Small group activity

Preparation: Each small group will need a copy of worksheet 8.1: *Values for sex,* and worksheet 8.2: *Values for sex cards.*

- Explain that sex can be something that builds people up or is 'life-giving'; it can also be something that breaks people down or is 'abusive' or 'life-limiting'. A person's attitude towards sex is often influenced by their approach to relationships in general.
- Give each small group the worksheet 8.1: *Values for sex* and worksheet 8.2: *Values for sex cards.*
- Ask pupils to sort the cards into the three columns headed 'life-giving behaviour', 'abusive behaviour' and 'could be either'.
- Give each group a few blank cards and ask them if they can think of any more actions for each column.
- Feedback to the group using the following questions:
  - Which cards were the most difficult to place? Why?
  - If appropriate, encourage personal reflection on how this discussion relates to pupils' relationships, sexual or otherwise.

Poster
Small group/whole class activity

- Ask each group to pick one example of behaviour that would make a relationship life-giving for those involved and one example of abusive behaviour that would make a relationship life-limiting for those involved.
- Give each group two pieces of A5 paper. Ask pupils to illustrate the two behaviours they have chosen on these pieces of paper, either by drawing a picture or writing a scenario.
- Collect all these cards up and use them to make a classroom poster of 'values for relationships and sex'.

Worksheet 8.1: *Values for sex*

The cards on worksheet 8.2 show different behaviours that might be seen in an intimate relationship. Sort the cards into the correct columns.

Live-giving behaviour	Abusive behaviour	Could be either

Worksheet 8.2: *Value for sex cards*

1 Listens to me carefully	**2** Ignores how I feel about things	**3** Respects my boundaries	**4** Challenges me to push my boundaries	**5** Pressurises me to have sex
6 Always lets me have my own way	**7** Thinks I am better than he/she is	**8** Compares me to his/her previous partners	**9** Is physically forceful towards me	**10** Puts my interests before his/her own
11 Wants to be with me all the time	**12** Is embarrassed of me in public	**13** Sees my good points and forgives the bad ones	**14** Challenges me to be a better person	**15** Is rude to me and puts me down
16 Works so hard that he/she is always tired	**17** Works hard to provide for all my needs	**18** Drinks too much all the time	**19** Makes sure I have a nice time as well as him/her	**20** Remembers my likes and dislikes
21 Sex within marriage	**22** Sex within a dating relationship	**23** Sex on a one-night stand		

Optional material

Changing bodies: Masturbation

This is an optional activity, which can be incorporated into SRE teaching at Key Stage 3 if felt appropriate. It is also included as an optional activity in the Key Stage 2 resources.

Some SRE resources and DVDs deal with this topic. We have therefore provided some optional material on this subject.

Young teenagers with access to the internet will have questions relating to masturbation. This lesson gives them the opportunity to think about this topic in a safe context. Through the suggested activities outlined below pupils will have an opportunity to discuss masturbation, as they reflect on Christian and other faith perspectives on this topic.

We recognise, however, that some schools and governing bodies may feel that masturbation is an unsuitable topic. If your school, in consultation with staff, governors and parents, deems it to be inappropriate, you may choose to omit this section.

Learning Objectives
- To consider what Christianity and other world religions think about masturbation

---

Learning Outcomes
- I can explain what Christianity and other world religions think about masturbation and give my own opinion

Lesson Resources
- Worksheet 9.1: *Masturbation statements*
- Worksheet 9.2: *Who thinks masturbation is...?*

Masturbation

20 minutes - Small group activity

Preparation

Each small group will need between six and nine different masturbation discussion cards from worksheet 9.1: *Masturbation opinions* (depending on students' age/ability). There are nine on the sheet. Each group will also need a copy of worksheet 9.2: *Who thinks masturbation is...?*

- Write a definition of masturbation on the board e.g. 'rubbing your genitals so that it feels nice'.
- Give each group cards from worksheet 9.1: *Masturbation opinions and worksheet 9.2: Who thinks masturbation is...?*
- Ask pupils to place each card at a point between the 'good' and 'bad' end of the line that reflects the opinion given.
- After pupils have placed all their cards, discuss what they have found.
    - Which opinion do you most agree with and why?

Plenary

10 minutes - Whole class activity

- Start class discussion with the following questions:
    - Why do you think people masturbate?
    - Can you suggest some times or places when/where it might be inappropriate to masturbate?
- Read out the following statement from the NHS website and ask pupils to do thumbs up/thumbs down to show whether or not they agree:
  'Masturbation can do you no emotional harm.'[13]
- Ask a few pupils to explain why they hold this opinion.

---

13. NHS, 'Is It normal To Masturbate? NHS [online], (15 January 2009). Available at http://www.nhs.ik/chq/Pages/1684.aspx?CategoryID=118&SubCategoryID=122 [accessed 1 September 2009].

Worksheet 9.1: *Masturbation opinions*

Krishna (Hindu)
Masturbation takes up time that could be better used for spiritual things.
Besides, you should learn to control your sex drive and not have it control you.

Hari (Buddhist)
One of our five moral teachings says you should avoid 'sexual misconduct'.
So every Buddhist has to work out for themselves whether it is OK to masturbate.

Marie (Christian)
I believe God gave me sexual desires so God understands when I masturbate.
I think it would be wrong if it became obsessive or it stopped me living a full life
to God's glory.

Ameena (Muslim)
The Qu'ran says that 'those who guard their virginity are free from blame'.
I think that masturbation is only OK if you do it to stop yourself committing a sexual sin.

Jasminder (Sikh)
I believe lust is one of the five vices, which stop you from reaching perfection.
It is hard to masturbate without lusting after other people.

Giovanni (Christian)
I believe that God made sex as a sacred act to bring you closer to your husband or wife.
If you use it any other way it will be less fulfilling. Also, it is hard to masturbate without
fantasising about another person and it can become addictive, so I try not to.

Fred (Agnostic – unsure whether there is a God)
I think masturbating is a good way of helping control your sex drive when you are
growing up. It is definitely better than sleeping around.

Chloë (Atheist – does not believe in a God)
Although no one talks about it much, most of my friends masturbate. There aren't any
health risks, but my doctor did say you can become addicted, so I try not to do
it very often.

Ruth (Jewish)
As an Orthodox Jew, I have been taught that the Talmud says that you should not waste
sperm, because it is meant for creating babies, so I don't think men should masturbate.
I am aware that other Jews may have different opinions.

Worksheet 9.2: *Who thinks masturbation is...?*

BAD

GOOD

Appendix 1

Values related questions for pupils to explore throughout KS3

Values are principles or convictions that act as a guide to behaviour. *All* schools promote a core set of values, which are shared and explored within the context of the school community. For church schools, these shared values will naturally be rooted in the wisdom and understanding of the Christian faith and particularly in gospel values. As students explore, question and experience these values, they are able to consider how Christian values are the same or different from the values of a 21st-century, secular society. They are also provided with a safe environment where they can consider the ways in which a particular value might be applied in a range of situations, and they can also grapple with controversial issues. Whilst the values listed below have been chosen as being distinctively Christian we recognise that many of these values will also be shared with community schools and those of other faiths.

For each value, a number of questions have been highlighted which relate specifically to relationships and sex education. Therefore, in order to support work undertaken in SRE, it is suggested that as each chosen value is explored within your school community, these questions are also considered and reflected upon – e.g. within individual subject areas; class tutorial time; collective worship; in staff discussion; and in discussions with key stakeholders. These questions will therefore be explored with students as they progress through their secondary education in an age-appropriate way.

Courage

Discuss times when you need to have courage to:

- Say no
- To share fears and worries
- Be yourself
- To ask questions
- To stand up for what is right.

Trust

- Who can I trust?
- Why should we be trustworthy?
- How do I maintain trust?
- What happens when trust is broken?

Consider aspects of:
- Being trustworthy
- Trusting in yourself.

Creativity

Explore the Christian belief that we are each unique and special – made in the image of God:
- Why am I unique and precious?
- How am I made in God's image?
- What am I here for?
- Who am I?
- Who made me?
- How is life a gift?
- How can I be a complete human being?

Justice

- Who loves me?
- How do we know what's right?
- Who is my neighbour?

Forgiveness

- When should I say sorry?
- How do I say sorry?
- Why do I need to receive forgiveness?
- How do I know when I should forgive?
- What changes when you forgive?
- How do you forgive yourself?
- How do you know that you are forgiven?

Peace

- Where do I feel comfortable and at peace? Which people make me feel at peace?
- How can I resolve conflict?
- How can I bring peace to others?
- What does peace mean to me?
- What makes me feel peaceful?

- Can I contribute to a peaceful community?
- Are there 'stages' in peace: peace within yourself; peace with close family friends; peace within the school community; peace within the local community; peace within a nation; peace between nations?

Friendship

- What is a friend?
- Who are my friends?
- How do I show friendship to others?
- How do I make friends?
- Why do I need friends?
- When do friends fall out?
- How do I maintain a friendship?

Humility

- What do I like about myself?
- How do I recognise my gifts?
- How do I feel when others are good at things?
- How do I put others before myself?

Truth

- How do I know who to believe?
- How do I tell the truth?
- Should I always tell the truth?
- Do I always respond positively to hearing the truth?
- Is truth different to different people?

Thanks

- What should I be thankful for – about myself? About others?
- How do I show my appreciation of others and myself?
- How do we celebrate who we are?
- How do we celebrate change?
- Who should I be thankful for?
- How do we celebrate milestones in our lives?

Compassion

- How do I become friends with those who are different to me? In what ways are people different to one another?
- How can I become a good listener?
- When should I be compassionate towards others and myself?
- What is it I love about myself? Why should I love myself?
- Can you think of times when 'your heart has gone out to somebody'? Did you act on this feeling?

Hope

- What do I hope for?
- What makes me feel 'hopeless'?
- Where do I see hope in the world?
- Who gives me hope?
- What do others hope for?
- How can I give hope to others?

Wisdom

- What steps can I take to help me make wise decisions?
- Which decisions in life require the most wisdom?
- Who helps me make important decisions?

Endurance

- What things are worth working for/at– even if we don't see immediate results?
- What/who might inspire and encourage me when I face difficulties in life?

Service

- What are my special gifts?
- How can I use these gifts to serve others?
- Does serving others mean that (don't take care of yourself or that I never assert myself?

Reverence

- How do I show respect and reverence to others?
- In what practical ways could a husband and wife show respect and reverence to one another?
- How do I treat other people when I disagree with them?
- How do I show respect to others?
- Would spending time in quietness and reflection help me when I have to make important decisions?

Koinonia

- Who helps and supports me?
- Which communities do I belong to?
- Who might help me in the future?
- What gifts do I share in the communities to which I belong – e.g. school; faith community; family; friendship groups; clubs/groups to which I belong?

Appendix 2

Sex and Relationships Education policy for use in Church of England secondary schools

This sample policy is based on SRE policy documents approved by Bristol and Salisbury diocesan boards of education for use in their church schools. It should be used as a template for the governing bodies of Church of England schools to discuss, amend and adopt, in the light of their unique school context. Following agreement on a school policy, it should be signed by the Chair of Governors. Notes to the policy are in italic text.

Sample Sex and Relationships Education policy

1   Introduction

1.1   *This school's SRE policy is based on the DCSF's Sex and Relationships Education Guidance.*

Sex education is part of the personal, social and health education curriculum in our school. We will teach within a framework of Christian values and the Christian understanding that sex is a gift of God as part of creation. Whilst we use sex education to inform young people about sexual issues, we do this with regard to matters of morality and individual responsibility, and in a way that allows students to ask and explore moral questions. (We have taken account of the guidance provided in teaching materials supplied by the Diocese.) Sensitivity and respect should be shown to all young people when teaching about personal relationships and sex education and SRE should be taught in a way that ensures that there is no stigmatization of young people based on their home/personal circumstances.

1.2 Context

All SRE in a Church of England school should be set in a context which is consistent with the school's Christian ethos and values.

- SRE should be based on inclusive Christian principles and values, emphasising respect, compassion, loving care and forgiveness.
- SRE should be taught in the light of the belief in the absolute worth of all people and the unconditional infinite love of God.
- SRE should reflect that sex is a gift from God as part of creation: a human longing for an intimate union.
- SRE should be sensitive to the circumstances of all children and be mindful of the variety of expressions of family life in our culture, yet it should also uphold the Christian values regarding relationships and marriage.

- Issues regarding human sexuality should be addressed sensitively.
- The exploration of reproduction and sexual behaviour within the science curriculum should stand alongside the exploration of relationships, values and morals and Christian belief.

Whilst students are given the opportunity to explore their own attitudes, values and beliefs and to develop an individual moral code that will guide their actions, this is exercised within an understanding of the right of people to hold their own views within a framework of respect for others.

2   Aims and objectives

2.1   We teach young people about:

- The physical development of their bodies as they grow into adults;
- The way humans reproduce;
- Respect for their own bodies and the importance of sexual activity as part of a committed, long-term and loving relationship;
- The importance of marriage and family life;
- Moral questions;
- Relationship issues;
- Respect for the views of other people;
- What they should do if they are worried about any sexual matters.

3   Principles

SRE should be based on the following principles:

- The sanctity of marriage is an important belief in Christian teaching and practice.
- Young people should learn the significance of marriage and families as key building blocks of community and society.
- Sex education includes learning about physical and emotional development.
- Young people will be taught the cultural and religious differences about matters of sexuality.
- Sex education is part of a wider social, personal, spiritual and moral education process.
- Young people should be made aware of the way in which advertising and the media influences their views about sexuality.
- Young people should be made more aware of the spiritual dimensions and joys of intimacy.
- Young people should be taught to have respect for their own and other people's bodies.
- Young people should learn about their responsibilities to others, and be aware of the consequences of sexual activity.
- Young people should learn that some people choose not to engage in sexual activity and that this choice should be respected and valued as a response to the gift of faith.
- Young people should be taught to understand the power of sexual desire.
- Young people should be made aware that sex can be used compulsively, competitively and destructively.
- Young people need to learn the importance of protecting themselves and of self control.
- Young people should be made aware of God's forgiveness and that there is always a way back.
- Young people should learn that it is important to build positive relationships that involve trust and respect.

- Young people need to learn how to keep themselves safe when using the Internet and other forms of technology.
- Young people need to be aware of responsible use of all forms of technology in order to respect the wellbeing and integrity of others.

4   The National Healthy School Standard

We now participate in the National Healthy School Standard scheme, which promotes health education. As participants in this scheme we:

- Consult with parents on all matters of health education policy;
- Train all our teachers to teach sex education;
- Listen to the views of the young people in our school regarding sex education;
- Look positively at any local initiatives that support us in providing the best sex education teaching programme that we can devise.

5   Organisation

5.1 We teach sex education through different aspects of the curriculum. While we carry out the main sex education teaching in our Personal, Social, Health and Economic (PSHE) education curriculum, we also teach some sex education through other subject areas (for example, science and PE, RE), where we feel that they contribute significantly to a young person's knowledge and understanding of his or her own body, and how it is changing and developing.

5.2 In PSHE we teach young people about relationships, and we encourage young people to discuss issues. We teach about puberty, what sex is, who it is for and the best contexts for intimacy, contraception, sexually transmitted infections, HIV and how to avoid life-limiting sexual choices. In PSHE we also teach about marriage and long-term stable relationships, reflecting on the variety of religious and cultural views held by people about these issues.

5.3 In science lessons, teachers inform young people about the human reproductive cycle, conception, pregnancy, foetal development and how these can be affected by diet, drugs and disease. For this aspect of the school's teaching, we follow the guidance material in the national scheme of work for science.

6   The role of parents

6.1 The school is well aware that the primary role in young people's sex education lies with parents and carers. We wish to build a positive and supportive relationship with the parents of children at our school through mutual understanding, trust and co-operation. In promoting this objective we:

- inform parents about the school's sex education policy and practice;
- answer any questions that parents may have about the sex education of their son/daughter;
- take seriously any issue that parents raise with teachers or governors about this policy or the arrangements for sex education in the school;
- inform parents about the teaching about sex education in school so that the parents and school can work together to support the young person with regard to sex education. We believe that, through this mutual exchange of knowledge and information, young people will benefit from being given consistent messages about their increasing responsibilities.

6.2   Parents have the right to withdraw their daughter or son from all or part of the sex education programme that we teach in our school. If parents wish their child to be withdrawn from sex education lessons, they should discuss this with the headteacher, and make it clear which aspects of the programme they do not wish their child to participate in. The school always complies with the wishes of parents in this regard.

7   The role of other members of the community

7.1   We encourage other valued members of the community to work with us to provide advice and support to young people with regard to health education. In particular, members of the Local Health Authority, such as the school nurse and other health professionals, give us valuable support with our sex education programme. Other people that we call on include local clergy, social workers and youth workers.

8   Confidentiality and safeguarding children procedures

8.1   Teachers conduct sex education lessons in a sensitive manner and in confidence. However, if a young person makes a reference to being involved, or likely to be involved, in sexual activity, then the teacher will take the matter seriously and deal with it as a matter of child protection. (This may be a matter for careful discernment if the disclosure reveals peer sexual activity.) Teachers will respond in a similar way if a child indicates that he/she may have been a victim of abuse.

If the teacher has concerns, he/she will draw the concerns to the attention of the designated teacher for child protection and safeguarding.
The headteacher will then deal with the matter in consultation with health care professionals. (See also Child Protection Policy.)

Advice for teachers on particularly sensitive issues such as female circumcision can be found at:
http://www.teachernet.gov.uk/wholeschool/familyandcommunity/childprotection

9   The role of the headteacher

9.1   It is the responsibility of the headteacher to ensure that both staff and parents are informed about our sex education policy, and that the policy is implemented effectively. It is also the headteacher's responsibility to ensure that members of staff are given sufficient training, so that they can teach effectively and handle any difficult issues with sensitivity.

9.2   The headteacher liaises with external agencies regarding the school sex education programme, and ensures that all adults who work with children on these issues are aware of the school policy, and that they work within this framework.

9.3   The headteacher monitors this policy on a regular basis and reports to governors, when requested, on the effectiveness of the policy.

10   Monitoring and review

10.1   The Curriculum Committee of the governing body monitors our sex education policy on an annual basis. This committee reports its findings and recommendations to the full governing body, as necessary, if the policy needs modification. The Curriculum Committee gives serious consideration to any comments from parents about the sex education programme, and makes a record of all such comments. Governors require the headteacher to keep a written record, giving details of the content and delivery of the sex education programme that we teach in our school. Governors should scrutinise materials to check they are in accordance with the school's ethos.

10.2 The SRE Policy has clear links with other school policies aimed at promoting pupils' spiritual, moral, social and cultural development, including the:

Equal Opportunities Policy

Health and Safety Policy

Inclusion Policy

Special Educational Needs Policy

Drugs Education Policy

PSHE & Citizenship Policy

Behaviour Policy

Anti-bullying Policy

Safeguarding/Child Protection Policy

ICT Policy and Safe Internet Use Policy

Confidentiality Policy

Signed:

Date:

SRE Policy: points to consider for staff and governors

Sex and Relationships Education in C of E secondary schools

The DCSF Sex and Relationship Education guidance states that Sex and Relationship Education (SRE) should be firmly rooted within the framework for Personal, Social, Health and Economic (PSHE) education and Citizenship. However, questions have been raised about how sex education should be taught within a church school setting – reflecting both the distinctive ethos and values which underpin a church school. In response to these issues the following guidance is offered to facilitate discussion when developing a policy.

Context

- SRE should be based on inclusive Christian principles and values, emphasising respect, compassion, loving care and forgiveness.
- SRE should be taught in the light of the belief in the absolute worth of all persons and the unconditional infinite love of God.
- SRE should reflect that sex is a gift from God as part of creation: a human longing for an intimate union.
- SRE should be sensitive to the circumstances of all children and be mindful of the variety of expressions of family life in our culture, yet it should also uphold the Christian values regarding relationships and marriage.

Guiding principles

In a Church of England school, Christian beliefs and values should underpin SRE, such that SRE is taught in the belief that:

- The sanctity of marriage is an important belief in Christian teaching and practice.
- Young people should learn the significance of marriage and families as key building blocks of community and society.
- Sex education includes learning about physical and emotional development.
- Sex education is part of a wider social, personal, spiritual and moral education process.
- Young people should be made aware of the way in which advertising and the media influence their views about sexuality.
- Young people should be taught to have respect for their own and other people's bodies.
- Young people should be taught to understand the power of sexual desire.
- Young people should be made more aware of the spiritual dimensions and joys of intimacy.
- Young people should learn about their responsibilities to others, and be aware of the consequences of sexual activity.
- Young people should be guided to understand the importance of building positive relationships with others, involving trust and respect.
- Young people should be made aware that sex can be used compulsively, competitively and destructively.
- Young people should be made aware of God's forgiveness and that there is always a way back.
- Young people need to learn the importance of protecting themselves and of self-control.

- Young people will be taught the cultural and religious differences about matters of sexuality.
- Young people should learn that some people choose not to engage in sexual activity and that this choice should be respected and valued as a response to the gift of faith.
- Young people need to learn how to keep themselves safe when using the Internet and other forms of technology.
- Young people need to be aware of responsible use of all forms of technology in order to respect the wellbeing and integrity of others.

Role of parents

The primary role in children's sex education lies with parents and carers. It is therefore important to build positive and supportive relationships with the parents and carers through mutual understanding, trust and co-operation.

Role of the local church and community

Members of the local health authority, such as the school nurse and other health professionals, are available to give support. In addition, the local church community can be a valuable resource in teaching about Christian marriage.

Role of the headteacher and governors

In a VA school the responsibility for the Sex and Relationships Education policy lies with the governors. The headteacher has to ensure that both staff and parents are informed about the school's sex education policy, and that the policy is implemented effectively. The governing body should carefully scrutinise teaching material to ensure it is appropriate for the school's distinctive ethos and foundation and that it is age-appropriate.

Confidentiality and safeguarding children procedures

Due regard should be given to Child Protection Policy in the development and delivery of SRE.

Questions to facilitate discussion

- How do we respect a wide range of individual beliefs and practices whilst upholding the Christian ideal of the sanctity of marriage?
- How can we equip young people to deal with the challenges of peer pressure?
- How can we enable young people to recognize that alcohol or drugs, for example, impede self-control and lead to actions which are later regretted? How do we help young people to explore the importance of self-control in their lives?
- In order to develop a healthy sexual relationship in later life, young people need to develop positive relationships, involving trust and respect. How do we help young people develop the skills necessary to achieve this?
- How can we help our young people protect themselves against sexual exploitation?
- How can the local church community be used as a resource for teaching about Christian marriage?
- What procedures are in place to monitor the governing body and headteacher's responsibilities for SRE?
- What provision can we make to encourage safe and responsible use of the Internet by our young people?

Appendix

Sex and Relationships Education: Working with parents

The DCSF guidelines for Sex and Relationships Education (SRE) state that: 'Schools should always seek to work in partnership with parents. This is essential to effective sex and relationships education.'[14]
Parents play a crucial role in educating their children about sex and relationships and also in helping them navigate the emotional and physical aspects of puberty. Through conversations, family ethos and the broad approach to life, young people pick up a significant amount of information about relationships from their parents. Despite this, many parents find it hard to talk to their children openly about sex and relationships. Schools are strongly encouraged to support parents in the important role they play, creating opportunity for discussion about the SRE curriculum and its implementation. It is important for parents to feel comfortable with a school's proposed SRE teaching and policy so that they are able to support their children in this aspect of their learning.
Currently, parents have the right to withdraw their children from SRE lessons taught as part of the PSHE and Citizenship curriculum, though only a very small minority choose to do so. If parents are concerned about SRE, arranging a meeting with them where they can discuss their concerns can be helpful.

Ideas for connecting with parents

There are numerous ways of connecting with parents before SRE lessons begin. Overleaf are a sample letter explaining this course and a suggested outline for a parents' evening. There is also a list of useful resources for parents, which can be downloaded from the Internet. It is suggested that parents are contacted well before the lessons begin to give them ample time to respond and build support for the course.

Parents' SRE letter
A good letter might include the following information:
- Which topics will be covered in which weeks so that parents can follow specific issues up at home;
- An explanation of the theology and philosophy behind the course;
- A recognition of the important role that parents play in SRE;
- An invitation to a parents' evening before the beginning of SRE lessons if appropriate.

Overleaf is a sample letter that might be sent to parents:

---

14. Department for Education and Employment, Sex and Relationships Education Guidance (0116-200) (DfEE, London, 2000), pp.25-26. Also see DCSF, Sex and Relationships Education Guidance 2010 (forthcoming).

[Date]

Dear

I am writing to inform you about the Sex and Relationships Education (SRE) that your son/daughter will receive during KS3 as part of their Personal, Social, Health and Economic (PSHE) education and Citizenship curriculum.

We are using, as a basis for our teaching in SRE, material from *Love and Sex Matters,* a new resource that has been produced with church schools in mind. It aims to give children and young people a safe environment within which they can explore different perspectives on sex and relationships.

The lessons present children with a variety of religious and non-religious viewpoints to allow them to make more considered decisions for themselves as they progress through adolescence. The resources also allow students to assess critically the messages they receive from the media and advertising. They encourage students to develop language suitable to discuss these often difficult subjects. The resources place a strong emphasis on the fact that healthy relationships are based upon people valuing both themselves, and other people. Themes explored include: the role of the media in shaping sexuality; what is love? why wait to have sex?; the emotional and spiritual aspects of sex; contraception; sexually transmitted infections; and an opportunity to reflect on how love and commitment can benefit the individual and the community, based on a Christian perspective.

We recognise that SRE can cause some parents concern. We also recognise that parents have an important role in teaching their children about sex and relationships, though many find it hard to talk openly about these areas. We would like to invite you to a parents' SRE evening on [date], when we will explain in detail the school's policy on SRE and the curriculum we are using. The evening will be interactive and discussion-based and there will be the opportunity for parents to ask questions and share their own perspectives. We do hope you will be able to attend this evening and actively support your children as they undertake SRE.

Yours sincerely,

[Name]

Parents' SRE meeting

Below is a suggested outline for an hour-long parents' meeting about the SRE curriculum.

Welcome (5 minutes)

It might be a good idea to start the evening off with some facts about what young people think about SRE or a funny film clip, e.g.:

- *SRE: Are You Getting It?:* (London, UK Youth Parliament), see www.ukyouthparliament.org.uk. A recent survey of young people's views of SRE.
- Excerpt from *Angus, Thongs and Perfect Snogging:* the first five minutes of the film show a comical scene between two parents and their teenage daughter.
- *Vox Pop on Love and Sex:* www.truetube.co.uk
- One of the numerous clips on BBC Bare Facts where children give their opinions on how and when parents should discuss sex: www.bbc.co.uk/barefacts

Small group discussion (15 minutes)

Ask parents, in small groups, to discuss the following two questions:

- What do you think SRE should cover?
- Do you think that parents have an important role in SRE?

Ask some of the groups to share the outcome of their discussions.

Presentation (15 minutes)

- Explanation of the school's SRE policy and SRE values framework (N.B. depending on the demographic of your school, it may also help to explain briefly a [the] Christian perspective[s] on sex.)
- Explanation of the theology and philosophy of this course, as outlined in the introduction.
- Explain and present one of the activities taken from *Love and Sex Matters* (for example, the card sorting from the summary activities).
- Explanation of the important role parents play in SRE, as outlined above.
- Tips for talking to children about sex and relationships (*Talk to Your Children About Sex and Relationships: Support for Parents* has some good guidelines – see below).

Question time (20 minutes)

- Invite parents to share any concerns they have about aspects of the policy, values framework or curriculum.
- Invite any further questions.

Resources for parents

There are leaflets for parents about SRE available for free download on the internet (see below). It is also good to give parents a copy of the school's SRE policy and SRE values Internet, so that they understand why SRE is taught as it is and are able to provide support as they feel is appropriate.

SRE & Parents Leaflet (0706 2001) (Department for Education and Skills, 2001), available at www.teachernet.gov.uk

Talk to Your Children About Sex and Relationships: Support for Parents (National Children's Bureau, 2003), available at www.ncb.org.uk

The NHS website has some guidance on talking to your children about sex, see http://www.nhs.uk/Livewell/Sexualhealth/Pages/Talktoyourteen.aspx or http://www.nhs.uk/chq/Pages/2341.aspx?CategoryID=62&SubCategoryID=66

The BBC website also has a section dedicated to helping parents talk to their children about sex, see www.bbc.co.uk/barefacts

Bibliography and Further Resources

Books and articles

Arnold, Johann Christoph, *A Plea for Purity: Sex, Marriage and God* (Plough Publishing House: New York, 1998)

Bell, Rob, *Sex God* (Zondervan: Michigan, 2007)

Brandon, Guy, *Just Sex* (Inter-Varsity Press: Nottingham, 2009)

Dunn, Judy & Layard, Richard, *A Good Childhood: Searching for Values in a Competitive Age* (The Children's Society: London, 2009)

Ecclestone, Alan, *Yes to God* (Darton, Longman & Todd Ltd: London, 1975)

Highton, Mike, *Difficult Gospel: The Theology of Rowan Williams* (SCM Press: Canterbury, 2004)

Kilbourne, Jean, 'Beauty … and the Beast of Advertising', *Media & Values* (No.49, winter 1990), available at www.medialit.org/reading_room/article40.html

Mason, Mike, *The Mystery of Marriage* (Multnomah Books: Colerado, 1996)

Sheldrake, Philip, *Befriending Our Desires* (Darton, Longman & Todd Ltd: London, 2002)

Williams, Rowan, *Lost Icons* (Continuum International Publishing Group Ltd: London, 2003)

Reports

Department for Education and Employment (now the DCSF), *Sex and Relationship Education Guidance* (0116-200), (DfEE, London, 2000)

House of Bishops' Group on Issues in Human Sexuality, *Some Issues in Human Sexuality: A Guide to the Debate* (Church House Publishing, London, 2003)

Macdonald, Sir Alasdair, *Independent Review of the Proposal to Make Personal, Social, Health and Economic (PSHE) Education Statutory* (Department for Children, Schools and Families (DCSF), London, 2009)

Teaching resources

Hope's Place has produced an eight-week course on self esteem for young women, Crowther, Joanna & Thomas, Elizabeth, *New I.D.* (2008), and a six-week course on identity for young men, Guthrie, Kate & Thomas, Dylan, *Man Up* (2009). See www.hopesplace.org.uk for more information.

Channel Four have a *Living and Growing DVD,* which many schools use as the basis of their PSHE education teaching.

Lovewise has a series of presentations on issues relating to SRE: *Choosing the Best, Growing Up … Growing Wise and Emotional and Physical.* See www.lovewise.org.uk for more information.

St Edward's RC School, Lees, Oldham, has developed an SRE resource for primary-aged children called *In the Beginning.* For more information, see the school website: www.st-edwards.oldham.sch.uk

Christian Action Research and Education send trained presenters into secondary schools to lead presentations. The programme is called *Evaluate: Informing Choice.* See www.evaluate.org.uk

Websites

www.4yp.co.uk
www.4ypbristol.co.uk
www.onesuffolk.co.uk/4yp
Websites for 4YP – sexual health and contraception services – for young people in Haringey, Bristol and Suffolk.

www.avert.org
Website of the charity Avert, an international AIDS charity, providing information about HIV and AIDS.

www.bbc.co.uk/religion
The BBC's webpages on religion.

www.bbc.co.uk/schools/gcsebitesize
The BBC's webpages on GCSEs; there is some useful information on religion and sex/relationships.

www.bbc.co.uk/barefacts
The BBC's webpages on talking to children about sex, love and relationships.

www.biblegateway.com
Website offering free access to many different versions and translations of the Bible.

www.brook.org.uk/
Website for Brook, which provides confidential sexual health advice for the under 25s.

www.checkyourbits.org
NHS website about STIs aimed at under-25s.

www.ChildLine.org.uk
Website of the counselling service for children, Childline.

www.drinkaware.co.uk
Website of the charity Drinkaware, providing information on alcohol, its effect on relationships, and on talking to under-18s about alcohol.

www.fpa.org.uk
Website of the sexual health charity FPA, which provides information, advice and support   to people across the UK on all aspects of sexual health.

www.healthyschools.gov.uk
Website of government initiative The Healthy Schools Programme.

www.kidshealth.org
Website created by Nemours, a non-profit organization, providing information for children, teens and parents on all aspects health including sexual health.

www.nationalstrategies.standards.dcsf.gov.uk
National Strategies website from the DCSF.

www.ncb.org.uk
Website of the charity National Children's Bureau.

www.nhs.uk
The National Health Service website with information on living healthily, including sexual health.

www.pshe-cpd.com
Website of the PSHE CPD programme for teachers and community nurses.

www.romanceacademy.org
The website for Romance Academy, which is a 12–15 week project supporting and mentoring up to twelve young people as they build their self-esteem, enhanced by sexual delay.

www.tcwp.co.uk
Website of the Christopher Winter Project, a training and consultancy company that provide sex and relationships education to young people, and training for teachers.

www.teachernet.gov.uk
Website for teachers and school managers.

www.truetube.co.uk
Website run by the charity CTVC providing and hosting media and text created by young people on a range of different topics to help start debates.

www.yourchurchwedding.org
The Church of England website about planning a church wedding.

Future *Love and Sex Matters*
Key Stage 3 resources

As part of the DCSF recommendations about Sex and Relationships Education to be implemented from September 2010 it is sugested that the topics of sexual orientation and homophobic bullying be covered at Key Stage 3.

These are the desired learning outcomes:
- Pupils will have considered the importance of respecting difference in relation to gender and sexuality.
- Pupils will have considered the unacceptability of prejudice and homophobic bullying.

In many church school contexts it is likely that Key Stage 3 will be deemed the appropriate time for this topic, in other contexts with consultation with governors and staff it may be thought more appropriate to cover these issues at Key Stage 4.
This is a matter for individual schools and governing bodies to decide.

Love and Sex Matters does not currently include a lesson plan and resources to assist in teaching this topic. However, resources on these topics are currently being developed, designed for use at either Key Stage 3 or Key Stage 4.

These resources will be available on the Salisbury Diocesan Board of Education website, www.saled.org, in early 2011.

Notes

Notes